MW01253410

I'll Never Forget Those Words
A Practical Guide To Death Notification

"There are many books available on grief and bereavement for professionals and the bereaved. Finally, the field has a volume that tackles the first moments of grief, where the stage is set for what will happen thereafter. Although the words of the death notifier may be a blur to some bereaved persons, for others they will certainly be the words that will never be forgotten. In either case, some comfort comes to the bereaved from knowing that at the start, someone treated them with respect and compassion at the worst of times…it is a very well done work and will certainly be welcomed by those working in the field who are responsible for death notifications."

Richard G. Tedeschi, Ph.D.
Professor of Psychology
UNC Charlotte
Charlotte, NC

"In this gem of a book, Lord and Stewart have provided a wealth of useful information to enable readers to grasp the dynamics of death notification and understand the reactions of loved ones and notifiers alike. They provide specific steps and practical guidelines to insure the most beneficial outcomes for all parties in this necessary but most challenging process."

Therese A. Rando, PhD, BCETS, BCBT
Author of *How to Go On Living When Someone You Love Dies*
and *Treatment of Complicated Mourning*

"I love this book! I congratulate Lord and Stewart for taking on this desperately needed endeavor. All notifiers should read it as well as supervisors and the people responsible for assigning notifiers and those who follow up with families."

Kathryn Turman, MSW
Director, Office for Victim Assistance
Federal Bureau of Investigation (FBI)

"Since families never forget how they were told of their loved ones' deaths, all notifiers should read this book so they won't regret the way they did it."

Dr. Dorothy Mercer
Professor of Clinical Psychology
Eastern Kentucky University

"Anyone who delivers death notifications should read this book! Lord and Stewart have put together an essential tool to empower those who deliver the sad news to do so with compassion."

M. Regina Asaro, MS, RN, CT
Coauthor of *Military Widow: A Survival Guide*

"*I'll Never Forget Those Words* is a much-needed guide for preparing professionals for the heart-rending and difficult task of notifying families of the death of their loved one. It is brief and practical, written in a straightforward, readable style, while clearly reflecting its scientific base. It will be valuable tool for death notification training."

Dr. Hannelore Wass
Professor of Educational Psychology
University of Florida

I'll Never Forget Those Words
A Practical Guide To Death Notification

Janice Harris Lord
Alan E. Stewart

Compassion Press
Burnsville, North Carolina

I'll Never Forget Those Words
A Practical Guide To Death Notification

Published by Compassion Press
A division of Compassion Books, Inc.

7036 State Highway 80 South
Burnsville, NC 28714
828-675-5909
www.compassionbooks.com

ISBN 978-1-878321-33-6

Library of Congress Control Number: 2008924364

Dedication

To those whose poorly managed notifications of the death of a loved one remain a source of suffering. May this book help ensure that others receive such news with more compassion.

Janice Harris Lord

To my wife and family, and in honor of the memories of Keith Emerson Clarke and Danny B. Newton

Alan E. Stewart

Contents

Acknowledgments

We both have been on the receiving end of poorly managed death notifications in our own families, and we both have worked professionally to help death notifiers improve their skills through training seminars and publications. More about our backgrounds can be found in About the Authors at the end of the book.

Our own experiences, however, are not so much the subject matter of this publication as are the experiences of others. The heart of the book is the personal stories of hundreds of notifiers and the notified who have shared painful parts of their lives with us, allowing us to draw conclusions about what helps and what hurts. We would never have been able to contribute to this narrow but very significant field of knowledge without partnering with them and their significant organizations.

We first acknowledge the national office of Mothers Against Drunk Driving (MADD) for allowing me, as their new Director of Victim Services in 1983, to begin exploring the death notifications of drunk driving crash victims. From that preliminary work, we gratefully acknowledge the U.S. Department of Justice's Office for Victims of Crime for engaging in a cooperative agreement with MADD a few years later to develop a curriculum on death notification for four professional groups: law enforcement, clergy and funeral directors, health care professionals, and victim advocates. These curricula were used by MADD advocates throughout the nation to reach thousands of notifiers and potential notifiers. Many of the cases discussed in this book were gleaned from those seminars. Most of the MADD training is now conducted by John Evans of MADD's national office, and he continues to gather and share notification stories from his seminars.

Our collaboration that led to this book began in 1997 when Alan was asked to evaluate the effectiveness of the MADD death notification training sessions so the model might be further refined. Even though both of us had attempted to stay abreast of other empirical studies related to death notification, we again conducted a literature review and incorporated new findings, which are included in Chapter I. We hope that the combination or our own work and studies with brief reviews of other work on the subject will enrich those who seek to provide compassionate notifications.

We are grateful to our editor and publisher, Bruce Greene, at Compassion Books in Burnsville, North Carolina, for undertaking this project and polishing our work. Diana Donovan and Allana Pettigrew assisted masterfully with line-editing.

We are especially grateful to the expert colleagues who reviewed an early draft of the book and made valuable suggestions. Most of them provided endorsement quotes printed herein, but we especially thank Dr. Dorothy Mercer from Eastern Kentucky University for her very thorough review as well as her support and assistance with this project for many years.

Most of all, though, we thank those who generously shared their personal notification experiences with us. They continue to inspire us and have helped us produce what we believe is a useful contribution to the death, trauma, loss, and victimology literature.

Janice Harris Lord
Arlington, Texas
April 2008

Introduction

Professional crisis responders and other caregivers do not choose their professions because it requires them to tell family members and friends that someone they love is dead. Sadly, however, lifesaving efforts sometimes fail, and the notification task falls to them.

Some who read this book will realize that they have done a good job with death notifications through their own instincts, even though they may not have been formally trained to do so. Others will welcome these suggestions on how to make death notifications competently and confidently.

First responders and health care professionals provide active and highly skilled services aimed to save lives. The goal of hospice professionals is to alleviate pain and stress through the dying process. Regardless of this intention, deaths happen. The most difficult notifications are generally those following sudden deaths. These deaths stem from vehicular crashes, violent crimes, suicides, accidents such as drownings or falls, and other unexpected causes. In these cases, those who valiantly try to save lives must suddenly shift gears and convey the tragic death information to families.

First responders typically called upon to notify include paramedics and emergency medical technicians, hospital emergency department physicians and social workers, and law enforcement officers and their victim advocates. Sometimes, others who may not have been directly involved in the trauma scene, such as medical examiners or coroners, police chaplains or the surviving families' own faith leaders make the notifications.

As notifiers prepare to perform this important task, questions inevitably arise. How should this task be done, when, where, and by whom? What else is involved besides telling of the death? What should be done if the person notified responds in a way that can bring harm to self or to others? Is it better to deliver the news and then just leave, or to remain for a while? How does a notifier best deal with his or her own feelings surrounding a death notification? What other complications might arise when death notifications are to be made in cultural and spiritual circumstances that differ from those of the notifiers?

Death notifications tend to be received as extraordinarily poignant events because they represent the beginning of a life without the loved one. Family and close friends don't forget death notifications. They may not remember every detail, but parts of the memory become permanently etched in their minds. If death notifications are delivered with care and compassion, the process can actually help surviving family members begin to grieve and make sense of the death. When death notifications are awkwardly delivered or poorly timed, when they convey wrong or contradictory information, or are made in a manner that the survivors find cold or unsupportive, they add to the pain and trauma the family must endure.

Death notifications are difficult for the notifiers as well. Most notifiers remember in vivid detail the first one they made. Even after years of experience, a notifier may find him or herself identifying with a particular family they are called to notify because that family may be much like their own family. This personal identification can lead to imagining what it would be like to die suddenly or tragically, and how their own death would impact their family. Notifiers may also absorb some of the post-death pain and trauma of the people they notify and not understand how to manage these feelings or reactions.

Despite the depth of potential negative effects of death notifications for both the notified and the notifier, few professionals receive training in death notification. There are several possible reasons. One is that death notification is only one of many complex skill sets that professionals must learn and administer. Death can feel like professional defeat, and the skills for handling it are not often formally developed or regularly practiced. Another reason is that professionals may see death notification as outside the boundaries of their practice. The law enforcement officer thinks the medical examiner should do it. The medical examiner assumes that the law enforcement officer did it. The emergency physician thinks the hospital social worker or chaplain should do it, while they in turn think it is the physician's responsibility. No one wants to do it, but someone must.

However, there are many things notifiers can do to facilitate healthy coping with the death, however, even while the notification is being delivered. *I'll Never Forget Those Words* has been designed to help fill this knowledge gap. While notification will never be a pleasant task, knowing that the receiving family has been treated the best way current knowledge knows to treat them can be satisfying.

The first goal of the book is to help readers understand the emotional value of a well-managed death notification. It is important to recognize the lasting effects of a death notification for both the survivors and for notifiers.

The second goal is to discuss what seem to be the essential elements of a helpful death notification based on the experiences of real people. Instead of providing a fixed, rigid model of death notification process, this book is designed to enable notifiers to plan for, and achieve, a notification that is responsive to the needs of the survivors.

The third goal is to help notifiers take care of their own emotional reactions during and after death notifications. Death notification will always be stressful and emotionally draining work. Appreciating this fact and recognizing negative and positive coping behaviors can contribute to long-term health and ensure that survivors, in their worst moments, receive the best the notifier can offer.

Chapter 1, "What We've Learned. . . and Not Learned about Death Notification," reviews the empirical literature pertinent to death notification. Although systematic inquiry about the best practices related to death notification has been scant, the existing resources do communicate the important, pivotal role that the notifier and the manner of notification play in the lives of the survivors. The literature also attests to the challenges and stresses associated with being a death notifier. Finally, the literature suggests that death notifications that leave survivors feeling unsupported, disrespected, or without answers to their questions (immediately following the death or afterward) contribute to negative outcomes that only add to the trauma. Research is still needed to determine the best methods of teaching death notification in a way that goes beyond knowledge to actual skill building. In addition, most of the empirical studies address notifier skills but fail to examine the reactions of those notified. Peers evaluating peers without surviving family input is obviously lacking in practicality.

Chapter 2, "Death Notification Practices," synthesizes the experiences of surviving families, professional groups, and researchers. It provides a way of thinking about how to deliver a death notification. Successful death notification is never a monologue presented by a notifier. It is an intense dialogue that begins with the notifier taking the lead and then relinquishing the leadership role to best meet the needs of the "family," whatever the make-up of that survivor group. Under chapter sub-headings that represent topics frequently arising in death notifications, this section of the book offers strategies to address the issues or challenges associated with each topic. Rather than a chronological model, Chapter 2 is designed as a template for developing one's own unique approach to making death notifications. Good death notification practice does not emerge so much from strict adherence to an outline as it does from using what is presented here to create notification processes focused on the survivors and what they need in order to feel appropriately informed, cared for, and supported.

Just as Chapter 2 addresses communication with survivors, Chapter 3, "Resilience Strategies for Notifiers," addresses coping strategies for the notifiers. The chapter encourages notifiers to examine their lives and how death notification work affects them. The chapter discusses a range of both healthy and unhealthy methods for coping with such stress. Tables given in the Appendix support how to remain resilient. One provides suggestions for emotionally recharging notifiers. Another gives a death notification coping strategy checklist that can help readers evaluate their own ways of dealing with the effects of death notification work. An extensive resource list offers readers multiple avenues of seeking support for families they want to help after the notification is given.

The book has been designed to be as informative and practical as possible for the many different kinds of professionals who deal with death. We hope it will educate new notifiers about death notification practice and help seasoned notifiers deal with difficult scenarios. Although we could have prepared a longer, academically oriented treatise to educate in the more traditional sense, we felt that such an approach would be less useful than a simple hands-on reference like *I'll Never Forget Those Words*, which includes many case examples drawn from our own experiences and those who have attended our seminars. The book does include a comprehensive review of the existing death notification scholarship, however. For this reason, we believe that *I'll Never Forget Those Words* will serve both as a hands-on guide and as an academic resource for informing research and practice.

1

What We've Learned . . . and Not Learned about Death Notification

On Valentine's Day 2005, shortly after nine o'clock in the evening, Deanna Salie heard a knock on the front door of her house in Fort Benning, Georgia. She got up from the couch, where she had been resting with a sick child, and opened the door to find two soldiers in dress green uniform standing on the front porch. As her eleven-year-old daughter listened, one of the notifiers began, "We regret to inform you . . ."

Deanna says she doesn't remember the words that followed because she was screaming and crying too loudly, but she has never forgotten those five words.

On Thursday evening, January 4, 2007, Dr. Harold (Hal) Engelke, a well-loved emergency physician and former national board chair of Mothers Against Drunk Driving (MADD), was sitting on his den sofa when he collapsed. His wife, Jane, a registered nurse, attempted resuscitation until an ambulance arrived. The paramedics pointed to a chair in the adjacent living room and told Jane to sit in it. Throughout their caregiving efforts they asked her nothing about her husband's health status or what had preceded the event. As they were leaving, one of them finally spoke to Jane and asked, "Do you have someone who can drive you to the hospital?"

Hal and Jane had devoted many hours to providing death notification training throughout the nation. Even so, Jane's experience at the hospital they had served for decades was less than optimal. She and her neighbors arrived soon after the ambulance, but the waiting area staff had not been alerted to their situation. They were first told to sit in the general waiting area. Then, as they started toward it, they were told instead to go to the private family room in the emergency area. No hospital staff joined them for almost half an hour. Finally, an emergency room physician, a stranger to them, walked in and stood a few feet away. He began the notification process by stating, "Your husband came in by ambulance …"

If first-response records had been communicated to the physician, he would have known that Jane was well aware of that. Without speaking of Hal's death, the physician began asking Jane questions about what Hal had been doing before he collapsed. A nurse stood behind him with a package of tissues. Frustrated with the process, Jane yelled, "He's dead, isn't he? I can see that! Do you think I'm stupid?" The physician turned, walked out, and did not return.

At that point, the nurses took over. Jane reports that they were very attentive and sensitive. Hal's body was cleaned and tubes were removed before their daughter and her family arrived. The nurses called the family's priest and secured a more private area for Hal's body. They offered Jane and the other family members ample time with him. The nurses provided refreshments and assigned a special nurse to address their needs. When she was ready, Jane went to the nurse's station, accompanied by her priest, and told a nurse which funeral home to notify. The nurse said he would take care of it right away and walked toward the phone. Jane and her priest rejoined the family.

By noon the next day, Jane was concerned that she had not heard from the funeral home, so she called to ask if there was a problem. It was then that she learned that the funeral home had not been called. When she phoned the hospital administrator for an explanation, he told her that it was her responsibility to call the funeral home, in essence blaming her for what had happened.

When the funeral director arrived at the hospital, the record of death had not yet been signed by the attending physician, so Hal's body still could not be released. The funeral director had to wait until another willing physician agreed to sign the paperwork.

(Even though the hospital inadequately handled the aftermath of Dr. Engelke's death, they conducted a meaningful memorial service honoring his life, including the unveiling of a memorial plaque, at the one year anniversary of his death. This event meant a great deal to his family and friends.)

In another city at another time, a police officer placed a yellow sticky note on a family's front door. The note instructed them to call the county morgue because their daughter had been killed. The note provided no information about how to call the morgue. The family

didn't understand why their daughter was at a morgue rather than at a hospital or funeral home. They had no idea how their daughter had been killed or how to contact the officer who left the note.

Death notification is not easy for the notifiers either. A medical examiner who works in a rural community in Washington State, where she knows many people, describes her reaction to phone calls requiring her services.

"Emotionally, I dread the pager or telephone call saying I have to go to work because I never know what I will find, who I will have to talk to, what their relationship to the decedent has been, or how they will handle the news of the death. Will I actually be the one to tell them? Or will someone else blurt it out to them in a moment of excitement/haste/panic/fear? … Then there are the times when I have known the deceased person. Physically, my stomach turns over and clenches. I feel a disconcerting rush as my adrenals kick in." (Schwartz 2003)

A young intern says he was nearly paralyzed with panic after his attending physician pronounced a young girl dead and told him to go to the waiting room to tell her family. Having received no education in death notification, he had no idea what to do or say.

A police officer describes in detail one of his first death notifications. As a rookie, he was riding with his supervisor when they were called to a "side-by-side" [in which they drive their vehicle to meet another officer so that they can talk window-to-window from their drivers' seats].

The officer in the other vehicle handed them a scrap of brown paper torn from a grocery sack. The scrap had an address written on it. He told them to notify the woman at this address that her father had just been killed. The supervisor passed the scrap of paper over to the rookie, saying, "Guess it's time you start doing these." With no more information than an address, and no training whatsoever, the rookie wondered what his supervisor would think of him if his anxiety became noticeable. Meekly, the rookie asked, "How do you do them?"

The supervisor grinned and replied, "I just walk up there and tell 'em. Then I get the heck out of there as soon as I can." The supervisor then tried humor to help the rookie with the task. "You know: 'I've got some good news and some bad news …' "

Years later, the officer can still describe how his heart felt stuck in his throat and how dry his mouth felt as he and his supervisor drove toward the woman's house. He remembers how he got out of the car and how the gate creaked when he opened it into her yard. He remembers how the grass poked up around the bricks of the sidewalk that led to her porch. He remembers the sound of his knocks on the frame of the locked screen door, which swayed a little with each knock. He remembers how desperately he hoped no one was home. He remembers the way the woman called out to ask who was there and what he wanted.

He told her he was a police officer. She opened her solid wooden door a little but did not unlock the screen door. She stood looking at him as he attempted to speak. He cannot forget how, from the other side of the screen door, he stumbled awkwardly through the notification, and how the woman screamed and then fainted. He called his supervisor for help. They broke through the screen door and dragged the woman to a stuffed chair in her living room, where the supervisor slapped at her face until she became conscious.

If the officer can still describe this death notification in so much detail, one can only imagine how vividly the woman remembers what happened before she fainted and after she regained consciousness.

Because death notification is one of the most difficult tasks professionals face, it is not unusual for notifiers to focus on their own anxiety and fail to recognize the full effect of notifications on surviving family members. How people learn about the deaths of their loved ones has profound implications for how they are able to cope in the aftermath (Leash 1994; Lord 2006; Stewart 1999).

The military is attempting to be more sensitive about delivering death notifications to families. Procedures are in place for all families to receive notifications in person, rather than through phone messages or telegrams. Protocols requiring stilted, formal language have been revised. Still, military families sometimes fail to be appropriately notified.

Among negative consequences of poor death notification is the filing of official inquiries and lawsuits.

On March 23, 2003, Marine Private Nolen Ryan Hutchings was killed in a friendly fire incident in Iraq as he traveled with an armored vehicle unit. His family was not notified of his death for twenty days, and they received the notification by phone rather than by a personal visit by Marine representatives as prescribed by military protocol.

They filed an official complaint with the Marine Corps. (Associated Press 2003)

On April 30, 2003, an Essex County, New Jersey, jury awarded $425,000 to a family that was first notified of the death of their daughter when they received a bill from the hospital for the shipment of her body to the morgue. The hospital had obtained the daughter's identifying information when she died, but failed to notify the family. After their daughter had been missing for twenty-nine days, the family filed a missing person's report. The verdict was awarded for the family's emotional distress from not having been notified. (BLUME et al. 2001)

Unfortunately, these scenarios illustrate that skillful, compassionate death notifications are far from universal. A variety of issues still contribute to problems surrounding death notification.

THE LIMITED RESEARCH

Since interest in death notification began developing about twenty-five years ago in advocacy groups like Mothers Against Drunk Driving and Parents of Murdered Children, only about thirty-five articles on the subject have appeared in professional and lay literature. Most of them are anecdotal or descriptive in nature. Only thirteen empirical studies of the death notification process have been published in peer-reviewed journals.

Resources for educating professionals about death notification practices did not emerge until the 1990s (Iserson 1999; Leash 1994; Lord 1997), and the authors had little more than their own experiences on which to rely. *I'll Never Forget Those Words* is the first book on the subject since that time.

Studies of Notified Families

The earliest empirical studies assessed the effects of viewing bodies in hospital emergency departments and found that the opportunity to view them when accompanied by a supportive and reassuring professional resulted in high satisfaction with the entire emergency department (Parrish et al. 1987).

Twenty sets of parents whose children had died unexpectedly were surveyed by Janzen, Cadell, and Westhues (2003). They observed that the following police behaviors were helpful during and immediately after the notification: (1) offering to contact friends and relatives, (2) driving the family to the hospital, (3) being thorough in the investigation of the death, (4) respecting the parents' wishes, (5) providing information, and (6) demonstrating empathy and sensitivity.

Studies of Law Enforcement Officers

A majority (67 percent) of a group of fifty law enforcement officers found death notifications "very stressful or extremely stressful" (Eth, Baron, and Pynoos 1987). The officers' apprehensions stemmed from (1) lack of training, (2) over identification with the family notified, (3) possibility of verbal or physical aggression on the part of the family, and (4) possibility of being negatively labeled by other officers if they had emotional difficulty with the task.

Studies of Physicians

Death notification among emergency physicians was evaluated by Swisher and colleagues (1993). The physicians uniformly reported that the death notification process was very stressful and they felt unprepared to handle it. Their stress was amplified if they also discussed tissue or organ donation with the family.

Another study of physicians (Knopp et al. 1996) revealed apprehensions about death notification similar to those of law enforcement officers. Physicians feared (1) being blamed for the death, (2) being inadequate to help with families' emotional reactions, and (3) being confronted with their own mortality and possibly similar deaths.

Ahrens and Hart (1997) surveyed 122 emergency physicians about their attitudes toward pediatric deaths. The physicians uniformly reported that notifications about child deaths were difficult with 66 percent stating that telling the family that a child had died was the most difficult task in emergency medicine. Only

14 percent of the sample had received any death notification training, and a mere 8 percent knew of any published recommendations for managing pediatric death notifications. The physicians further reported feeling guilty or inadequate following pediatric death, with 47 percent of them continuing to feel impaired by the death notification experience at least for the remainder of their shifts.

Between 1994 and 2000, Benenson and Pollack (2003) evaluated seventy emergency-duty residents on death notification skills, after finding that only 12 percent of the residents (who represented twenty-eight U.S. medical schools) had received any death notification training. Before being evaluated, the residents were given a one-hour lecture followed by a ten-minute simulated scenario. The researchers found that third-year residents and female residents were the best notifiers. The ratings were based on (1) use of appropriate terms (dead, died, death), (2) brief, clear explanations of the sequence of events, (3) attempts to comfort the family and answer questions, and (4) appearance of equanimity. The researchers concluded that effective death notification training should incorporate (1) didactic information, (2) demonstration, and (3) role play. They also concluded that their teaching method would help physicians if incorporated into emergency medicine curricula.

Hobgood and colleagues (2005) developed a death notification acronym for emergency physicians: **GRIEV_ING**, which stands for the following death notification steps.

Gather all family members;
(Call) **R**esources such as chaplains, family, and friends;
Identify yourself and use the name of the deceased person;
Educate the family about what happened;
Verify the death by using the appropriate terminology;
_ Give the family personal space and time to absorb the information;
Inquire if there are questions and attempt to answer them;
Nuts and Bolts (discuss organ donation, funeral services, personal belongings, viewing of the body);
Give the family your contact information and offer to answer more questions as they arise.

Before teaching their acronym to twenty emergency medicine residents, the researchers pretested them on self-confidence, communication skills, and competency in delivering death notifications. They then trained the residents in the **GRIEV_ING** model during a two-hour time frame that included presentation of the model, small group discussion, and paired role play. Over the three months following the training they tested the trained residents on the same criteria. Significant improvement was noted immediately after the training when compared to notifications beforehand, but no additional improvement was achieved over the next three months.

Hobgood later worked with a different group of researchers and looked at the results from teaching the **GRIEV_ING** model to a group of emergency medicine residents, including not only role-playing but also structured feedback. They compared these results with another group whose training included no feedback. They found that teaching the model significantly improved death notification competence, but that feedback on the role plays did not help (Hobgood et al. 2007).

Studies of Military Notifiers

One study found that the more often survivor assistance officers (SAOs) in the army were exposed to the acute distress of the survivors they notified, the more they experienced negative reactions like a diminished sense of well-being and various physical symptoms (Bartone et al. 1989). The researchers observed that when notifiers had higher levels of dispositional hardiness (the ability to endure stress without becoming physically ill) and social support, they had less reactive distress.

Later, Ender and Hermsen (1996) also studied army SAOs. The officers indicated that neither military notification procedures nor their training in those procedures adequately addressed the complexities of the military notification scenarios they faced, including how to handle their own emotional reactions. These reactions included, for example, sorrow because of identification with the survivors and grief over memories of their own previous losses. The SAOs were further challenged by nontraditional families they had to notify—single parents, for example, or broken or blended families. Their guidelines were unclear about whom to notify as significant others. Cultural differences presented additional challenges that were not included in standard procedures. The researchers pointed out that racial and ethnic differences between the SAOs and the survivors significantly compromised the officers' ability to provide appropriate support.

Studies of Mixed Populations

While preparing to write his book *Death Notification: A Practical Guide to the Process*, Leash (1994) surveyed 400 people in the Sacramento area about their notification experiences, but included no family members who had been notified that a loved one had died. The survey included 200 health care professionals exposed to traumatic injury and death on a daily basis, 100 college students in a class on death and dying, and 100 family members and friends of someone who had been injured or became suddenly seriously ill. All were asked their opinions about how death notifications should be handled. The overwhelming majority (90.3 percent) felt that the family should be notified of the death immediately, regardless of the time of day or night. A slight majority (58 percent) preferred notification by phone over driving to the hospital to be told. By a slightly narrower margin, 55 percent of the study participants preferred being notified by phone, by someone from the hospital, over notification in person by law enforcement officers. (More of the study participants supported officer notification when the death was unexpected, however.)

Leash felt that the resistance to law enforcement notification could have been related to the study participants' belief that hospital personnel would be better trained. He hypothesized that this attitude could change as more officers receive death notification training.

In scenarios where the family did go to the hospital, 73.3 percent said they felt the notification should be made by the physician rather than by a chaplain, nurse, or social worker. Most indicated that families should be able to view the body as soon as possible, after it was properly cleaned. They felt that notifiers should answer questions about the death without distorting or withholding information. They felt that how and when the survivors were notified was significantly more important than where and by whom they were told.

The authors of *I'll Never Forget Those Words* and one of their colleagues examined the death notification experiences of 245 death notifiers (Stewart, Lord, and Mercer 2000). The respondents in the study represented fourteen professions categorized generally as (1) law enforcement, (2) clergy, (3) mortuary professionals, (4) health care professionals, (5) mental health professionals, and (6) victim assistance providers. The professionals surveyed had recently received death notification training in a classroom and experiential framework, sponsored jointly by Mothers Against Drunk Driving and the U.S. Department of Justice's Office for Victims of Crime. The study was conducted, in part, to inquire about participants' past experiences of death notification and to assess the value of the MADD training.

Across the six professional groupings, clear consensus emerged that death notification of violent crimes placed the greatest emotional demands on the notifiers. Notifications of suicides ranked a distant second, followed by notifications of automobile crash deaths related to drunk driving. These three types of deaths result from harmful intent or reckless negligence. All are someone's fault.

The next three rankings involved truly accidental deaths. The death of a child by any cause was ranked as the fourth most difficult type of notification. Many of the study participants wrote details of child death notifications that were especially difficult for them. Other researchers have pointed out that the death of a child represents a reversal of the expectation that parents are supposed to die before their children (Cleiren 1992; Rando 1993). The fifth-ranked difficult death notification category was that of accidental deaths of a non-child of any age, with such causes as drowning, falls, and drug overdose. Finally, vehicular crash deaths not caused by drunk driving ranked closely behind child and accidental deaths.

In addition to their ranking of the effects of types of death notification situations on the notifiers, this group of notifiers rank-ordered the reactions of surviving family members in terms of how difficult they were for notifiers to manage. Aggressive and destructive behaviors (toward either self or others or both) were by far the most difficult for the notifiers. They reported that family members had smashed or thrown things out of anger or helplessness. Others had physically attacked someone they felt to be responsible. Still others had struck the notifier. The notifiers had to decide how far they could let these reactions go before attempting to deflect or stop the behavior, and they often had to make that decision quickly.

The second-ranking stressor was expressions of intense anxiety and uncontrollable crying on the part of family members. The notifiers felt they should know how to provide comfort, but they did not.

The Lack of Death Notification Education

With the possible exception of mortuary professionals, most people who deliver death notifications receive no curriculum-based education on how to perform the task or how to react to traumatized or grieving persons (Hodgkinson and Stewart 1998; Kaul 2001; Stewart and Lord 1999). In the previously mentioned MADD study, 41 percent of the 245 notifiers had received neither classroom education nor experiential training in death notification before attending the MADD seminar (Stewart, Lord, and Mercer 2001). The respondents reported that before the MADD seminar, their greatest needs included (1) specific detail about how to perform death notifications—how to phrase introductions, how to word the actual notification statement, what to say and do after the statement, (2) how to respond to the emotional reactions of the survivors after the notification, (3) how to manage their own emotional reactions both during and after the notification, and (4) how to use other personnel to help.

Future research needs to include assessment of notifiers' needs as well as the long-term benefits of curriculum-based death notification training with and without experiential components. (Benefits of training tend to include greater job satisfaction, fewer employment assistance referrals, and fewer turnovers, but more data is needed) In addition, the most significant need is to identify helpful and hurtful aspects of notification on survivors and to compare the impact of death notification on survivors when delivered by trained versus untrained notifiers.

THE NEED FOR DEATH NOTIFICATION EDUCATION

Increasing Cultural and Spiritual Diversity of the United States

Unless the deceased's family receives the notification from their primary care physician or faith leader, the information is usually delivered by a stranger. This stranger, whether a police officer, an emergency physician, a paramedic, or a medical examiner or coroner, may have little understanding of the social, cultural, or religious perspectives of the family. Education on how best to deliver death notifications to those with cultural and spiritual practices different from those of the notifier can help ease the discomfort of these difficult situations.

The United States is rapidly becoming more culturally diverse than in previous generations. The total number of immigrants living in the United States reached an all-time high of 37.5 million in 2006, an increase of 16 percent in 5 years (Population Reference Bureau 2007).

Along with cultural diversity comes religious diversity, which is extremely relevant to death notification. Spiritual and religious diversity in the United

States has also significantly increased. While the United States does not include a question about religion in its census, various experts have made reasonable estimations. For example, Kosmin and Lachman (2002) estimate the following changes occurred between 1990 and 2000.

- The number of Muslims in the United States more than doubled to over 1 million, with about 65 percent being foreign-born. An official State Department fact sheet cites Power (1998), however, who stated that Islam is by far the fastest growing religion in the United States. Power estimated that by the year 2010, the U.S. Muslim population will increase to 4 to 6 million, which will cause it to surpass the Jewish population.
- The number of Buddhists increased by 170 percent to reach more than 1 million living in the United States.
- The number of Hindus increased by 237 percent to total more than 1 million in this country.

In order for a death notification to be delivered sensitively and compassionately, the notifier must speak the same language as the family; and if possible, at least one of the notification team should be a spiritual leader from the family's own faith.

To briefly illustrate the significance of cultural and spiritual sensitivity, it may be useful to know that most traditional Buddhists attempt to detach themselves from expectations and outcomes in order to accept "what is." Their efforts to remain calm and non-reactive during a notification may seem strange to someone with no knowledge of Buddhism. It is also important to Buddhists that proper prayers are offered over the body of their loved one immediately, in a serene atmosphere, to assist the spirit in departing from the body.

Since September 11, 2001, many from the Middle East, especially Muslims, may become anxious in the presence of law enforcement officers out of fear of deportation. In addition, Muslims have religious prohibitions that can affect death notification practices. Muslim women who cover their hair do not allow men to enter their homes unless they are covered and their husbands are present. This presents a dilemma if the notifier is a male law enforcement officer who expects to enter the home. In addition, within Islam, outward manifestations of grief are strongly discouraged because of their belief that Allah preordains one's time of death. Notifiers unaware of these beliefs and practices might conclude that surviving family members are not reacting appropriately and, in an extreme situation, they might even falsely conclude that a family member may be responsible for the death.

There is more information on cultural differences surrounding death, dying, and death notification among the six major world religions (Native American spirituality, Hinduism, Buddhism, Judaism, Christianity, and Islam) in *Spiritually Sensitive Caregiving: A Multi-Faith Handbook* by Lord and others (2008).

The Difficult Effects of Death Notifications on the Notifier

Just as it takes a certain kind of person to be a good law enforcement investigator, therapist, or faith leader, it takes a certain kind of person to be an effective death notifier. A dramatic switch of traditional roles is necessary, particularly for health care professionals (other than hospice workers) and law enforcement officers. These professionals are trained to protect and maintain life by thinking quickly and intervening actively. Language and behaviors can become chaotic in their valiant efforts to save lives or apprehend suspects. To achieve their professional goals, officers and physicians are trained to disengage or repress their emotional reactions so they can work clearly and objectively.

Thus, when a criminal offender's actions result in a death, law enforcement officers tend to interpret their efforts as a failure, even when they are able to apprehend the criminal. Police are trained to control other people's behavior through any means, including the use of deadly force when necessary. Calm, gentle, overtly caring support like that required for a death notification is the exact opposite demeanor to that required for most other law enforcement duties. As one law enforcement officer who attended a MADD seminar said, "Death notification is not a 'call for service.' The needs of the person served are radically different." Said another, "It is our duty to be sure that those we are sworn to serve have the best of us at their worst of times."

When physicians lose lives after providing emergency care, resuscitation, or even long-term care, they too may feel they have failed. In addition, fiscal limitations within many emergency departments require that physicians and nurses accomplish more in less time than only a few years ago. This puts pressure on medical staff to made death notifications while under pressure to treat the next patient. While a collaborative approach to dealing with surviving family members is ideal, it is seldom practiced. Useful recommended practices for death notification are surprisingly lacking (Iserson 1999; Kaul 2001; Leash

1994; Stewart, Lord, and Mercer 2000; Stewart, Lord, and Mercer 2001). For example, in a hospital waiting area, a physician hurriedly and formally told a family that their son/brother had "expired." The deceased's adolescent brother became very upset and hit the physician in the face, knocking off his glasses. Rather than understanding that this is a fairly natural reaction and attempting to support the boy, the physician tried to restrain him and eventually filed a personal injury lawsuit against him. Training that includes information on common reactions like this might have helped the physician to respond differently.

Paramedics and EMTs are also called upon to respond quickly, treat appropriately, and transport safely; their primary goal is to save lives. Distress results when the mission fails. As one emergency worker proclaimed, "Nobody is going to die in my ambulance" (Pechal 2003). Making the transition from valiant protector or healer to that of death notifier clearly places extraordinary demands on these professionals (Stewart 1999; Swisher et al. 1993).

Failure to Recognize the Need for Effective Death Notification

Wass (2004) suggests that institutions generally resist offering death education programs. Her research finds that they rarely acknowledge the need for these programs. When the need goes unrecognized, few or no resources are committed to training, and both the notified and the notifier suffer as a result.

This is partly a result of the lack of a full body of empirical research. Even though such empirical research is limited, there is ample evidence to show that how people learn about the deaths of their loved ones can have significant implications for their coping ability (Leash 1994; Lord 2006; Stewart 1999) and that death notification education helps them do a better job.

EXPERIENTIAL EXERCISES

Those who have not yet delivered a death notification may benefit from remembering their own personal experiences of being notified of the deaths of family members or friends, and are encouraged to respond to the first two sets of questions below.

Persons with experience as notifiers will probably recognize the impact of death notifications from their own experiences, but they may not have thought of their insights as a learning exercise. They are encouraged to respond to all three sets of questions below.

My First Experience in Receiving a Death Notification

1. What was the first death you remember? (It may have been the death of a pet, a grandparent, another child ...)
2. Do you remember who told you and how?
3. How did you react?
4. How well did your outward, public behavior reflect the way you felt inside?
5. What, if anything, kept you from expressing how you felt?
6. How well did the information you were given match what you wanted to know?
7. What questions did you have about the death that went unanswered?
8. What conclusions did you draw from the questions that were either not answered or were inadequately answered?
9. What parts of the notification do you think were handled well?
10. Why do you think you still remember this notification?
11. How do you wish it had been handled differently?
12. What from that experience will you use in delivering notifications yourself?

My First Experience in Receiving a Trauma-related Death Notification

1. Who told you about this sudden or traumatic death?
2. What details do you remember about the notification?
3. What information about the death did you want but not receive?
4. How did you react to the notification?
   (a)... when it was made?
   (b)... a week later?
5. What are your emotional reactions to it now?
6. How does your body feel as you think about it now?
7. What parts of the notification do you think were handled well?
8. Why do you think you still remember this notification the way you do?
9. How do you wish it had been handled differently?
10. What from that experience will you use in delivering notifications yourself?

The First Death Notification I Delivered

1. Who told you to deliver the notification?
2. How did you react?
3. Did you have enough details to answer the family's questions?
4. What about it do you remember the most?
5. What parts of the notification do you think you handled well?
6. Why do you think you still remember this notification the way you do?
7. How do you wish it had been handled differently?
8. What from that experience has helped you deliver more appropriate notifications since that time?

All death notifications are difficult for survivors, even when the death is expected in a hospital or hospice setting. In these situations, telling the family that the death is expected may be more traumatic than the actual death pronouncement. When the death is sudden, however, the death notification represents the survivors' first information about it. It is more than a "loss." It is, for most, a traumatic, life-changing event.

No death notification is exactly like another because so many variables are involved. The next chapter is designed to shed light on different death notification cases in order to address many aspects of death notification. No one should use one uniform script for notification. Memorized statements often come across as too formal. For this reason, Chapter 2 offers practical tools and recommendations to use as the need arises.

REFERENCES FOR CHAPTER 1

Ahrens, W. R., and R. G. Hart. 1997. Emergency physicians' experience with pediatric death. *American Journal of Emergency Medicine* 15:642–643.

Associated Press. 2003. Marines' handling of death notification draws lawmaker's complaint. *The Post and Courier* (Charleston, SC: April 16). Retrieved 08/02/03 from http://www.postandcourier.com/stories/041603/sta_16demint.shtmlm.

Bartone, P. T., R. J. Ursano, K. M. Wright, and L. H. Ingraham. 1989. The impact of a military air disaster on the health of assistance workers. *Journal of Nervous and Mental Disease* 177:317–328.

Benenson, R. S., and M. L. Pollack. 2003. Evaluation of emergency medicine resident death notification skills by direct observation. *Academic Emergency Medicine* 10, no. 3 (March): 219–223).

BLUME GOLDFADEN BERKOWITZ DONNELLY FRIED & FORTE. 2001. $425,000 verdict for delay in death notification. Verdicts/Settlements (Spring). Retrieved 08/02/03 from http://www.njatty.com/articles/medmal/mzsp01b.html.

Cleiren, M. 1992. *Bereavement and adaptation: A comparative study of the aftermath of death.* Washington, DC: Hemisphere.

Ender, M. G., and J. M. Hermsen. 1996. Working with the bereaved: U. S. Army experiences with nontraditional families. *Death Studies* 20:557–575.

Eth, S., D. A. Baron, and R. S. Pynoos. 1987. Death notification. *Bulletin of the American Academy of Psychiatry Law* 15:275–281.

Hobgood, C., D. Harward, K. Newton, and W. Davis. 2005. The educational intervention "GRIEV_ING" improves death notification skills of residents. *Academy of Emergency Medicine* 12:4296–4301.

Hobgood, C., D. Hollar, P. Woodyard, and S. Sawning. 2007. Teaching death notification skills to emergency medicine residents: The role of feedback. *Academy of Emergency Medicine* 14, no. 5, Suppl. no. 1, S77.

Hodgkinson, P. E., and M. Stewart. 1998. *Coping with catastrophe: A handbook of post-disaster psychosocial aftercare.* 2nd ed. London: Routledge.

Iserson, K. V. 1999. *Grave words: Notifying survivors about sudden, unexpected deaths.* Tucson: Galen Press.

Janzen, L., S. Cadell, and A. Westhues. 2003. From death notification through the funeral: Bereaved parents' experiences and their advice to professionals. *Omega: Journal of Death and Dying* 48:149–164.

Kaul, R. 2001. Coordinating the death notification process: The roles of the emergency room social worker and physician following a sudden death. *Brief Treatment and Crisis Intervention* 1:101–113.

Knopp, R., S. Rosenzweig, E. Bernstein, and V. Totten. 1996. Physician-patient communication in the emergency department, Part I. *Academic Emergency Medicine* 3:1065–1069.

Kosmin, B., and S. Lachman. 2002. *Top twenty religions in the United States.* New York: City University of New York. Retrieved 12/06/07 from http://www. adherents.com/rel_USA.html#religions.

Leash, R. M. 1994. *Death notification: A practical guide to the process.* Hinesburg, VT: Upper Access.

Lord, J. H. 1997. *Death notification: Breaking the bad news with compassion for the survivor and care for the professional.* Washington, DC: U.S. Department of Justice, Office for Victims of Crime; and Irving TX: Mothers Against Drunk Driving.

Lord, J. H. 2006. *No time for goodbyes: Coping with sorrow, anger, and injustice after a tragic death.* 6th ed. Burnsville, NC: Compassion Press.

Lord, J. H., M. Hook, S. Alkhateeb, and S. English. 2008. *Spiritually sensitive caregiving: A multi-faith handbook.* Burnsville, NC: Compassion Press.

Parrish, G. A., K. S. Holdren, J. J. Skiendzielewski, and O. A. Limpkin. 1987. Emergency department experience with sudden death: A survey of survivors. *Annals of Emergency Medicine* 16:792–796.

Pechal, T. 2003. Emergency rescue workers dealing with death. *The Forum (Association of Death Education and Counseling)* 29 (3): 5. Retrieved 2/29/08 from http://www.adec.org/publications/forum/0307.pdf.

Population Reference Bureau. 2007. Retrieved September 15, 2007 from http://www.prb.org/countries/UnitedStates.aspx.

Power, C. 1998. The new Islam. *Newsweek*, March 16, 34. Retrieved 12/06/07 from http://www.islamfortoday.com/historyusa4.htm.

Rando, T. A. 1993. *Treatment of complicated mourning.* Champaign, IL: Research Press.

Schwartz, M. 2003. Investigating deaths in the field. *The Forum (Association for Death Education and Counseling)* 29 (3): 1, 3–4. Retrieved 2/29/08 from http://www.adec.org/publications/forum/0307.pdf.

Stewart, A. E. 1999. Complicated bereavement and posttraumatic stress disorder following fatal car crashes: Recommendations for death notification practice. *Death Studies* 23:289–321.

Stewart, A. E., and J. H. Lord. 1999. Evaluation research finds MADD death notification seminars effective. *MADDvocate*, Winter, 16–17.

Stewart, A. E., J. H. Lord, and D. L. Mercer. 2000. A survey of professionals' training and experiences in delivering death notifications. *Death Studies* 24:611–631.

Stewart, A. E., J. H. Lord, and D. L. Mercer. 2001. Death notification education: A needs assessment study. *Journal of Traumatic Stress* 14:221–227.

Swisher, L. A., L. Z. Nieman, G. J. Nilsen, and W. H. Spivey. 1993. Death notification in the emergency department: A survey of residents and attending physicians. *Annals of Emergency Medicine* 22:102–106.

Wass, H. 2004. A perspective on the current state of death education. *Death Studies* 28:289–308.

Notes

2

Death Notification Practices

Since no two death notifications will ever be exactly alike, attempting to conduct a death notification according to a rigid, memorized protocol rarely helps the notifier, and it can come across as cold and unfeeling to the family (Lord 1997). This chapter includes many actual death notification cases, some handled well and some not, and several discussion questions. The suggested practices, developed from interviews with hundreds of surviving family members and notifiers, should help you manage the process well. As any given notification unfolds, however, you should always use your own best judgment about when, or if, to use specific practices.

As noted previously, some family members experience complicated and difficult grieving processes because they cannot dismiss the way their notification of death was handled. Certain aspects of the death notification stay with them for their lifetimes because in high-stress situations the neurotransmitter norepinephrine is pumped into the brain, activating it for the fight, flight, or freeze response. Adrenaline also causes the brain to store emotional reactions for long-term memory. This is why human beings tend to remember certain aspects of highly emotional events so vividly and why learning competent death notification process is so important.

Despite the notifiers' best intentions, poorly presented death notifications can happen in all professions because of lack of training and/or emotional issues that notifiers have about death or loss in general. We hope that this chapter will help notifiers to understand why some are less than successful and how to have better results in the future.

THE IMPORTANCE OF COMPASSION

Compassion is mentioned throughout this book as a central goal in delivering death notifications, yet it is not a comfortable or familiar word for many of those called upon to perform this difficult task. It is not a word commonly spoken in law enforcement academies, nor is it frequently used in emergency medicine textbooks. It is thought by many to be the language of social workers and theologians.

The literal meaning of "compassion," according to Webster's, is "with passion." The first definition of "passion" has to do with suffering, the enduring of pain. Back to theology, "compassionate" is one of the adjectives often used to describe God in the Hebrew Bible, the New Testament, and the Qur'an. A compassionate God or a compassionate human has feelings about the suffering of others. A compassionate person does not shut off emotional reactions, as may be required in apprehending a criminal or performing surgery. For death notification, it implies caring about the suffering being inflicted on others and continuing to care in the aftermath through providing competent services.

THE BASICS OF DEATH NOTIFICATION

A competent and compassionate death notification begins with collecting accurate information and planning carefully who will be involved in the notification process. It includes paying attention to unique circumstances of each death that can affect where, when, and how the notification is made. It includes planning key components of what will be said during the notification. Once the actual notification is given, the process is still far from complete. It includes careful attention to the family's reactions and may include giving information about organ/tissue donation, viewing the body, and information about funerals, burial, and, in some cases, law enforcement investigations. A bond is usually created between the notified and the notifier. The quality of that bond can either create an emotional safety net for the family or cast a shadow that can negatively penetrate future efforts to help.

Collect Accurate Information

Basic information such as identity must be accurate, even though making the notification in a timely manner can make it difficult to get all the information the family may want (Stewart 1999). When the death occurs in the home with hospice care, or in the hospital or other facility where identity verification and interaction with the family has been ongoing, there is no question about the identity of the person who died. Sometimes, when the body is heavily damaged, even family members are not sure of the identity. In other situations, it is crucial that complete and accurate information be obtained before the notification is given.

Experiential Exercise

In the following exercise, true experiences of families illustrate the significant nature of this aspect of death notification. Imagine yourself as the person notified in each of these situations and describe how you think you might have reacted.

- A family in Hillsborough County, Florida, was notified by law enforcement that their son had been killed, but the notifying officer did not know the time or circumstances of the death or where their son's body had been taken.
- In Dallas, Texas, a couple was notified that their "son and his friend" had been killed by a drunk driver while on military duty. No names were given.
- At seven o'clock one morning, a man went to the door and was handed a note from an officer. The note instructed the man to call a Tallahassee phone number.
- In another Texas case, a police officer handed a man a note that read, Call the medical examiner's office in Dimton." A phone number followed this sentence with its mysterious town name.

Here is what happened to these families:

In the first case, the parents contacted funeral homes the next morning until they found the one to which their son had been taken. They were told that their son had lived for eight hours after they were informed of his death. They therefore had missed the opportunity to say good-bye at the hospital while he was still alive.

In the second case, after numerous calls, the family learned that it was their daughter (who was also in the military) and a friend, not their son, who had been killed.

In the third case, the father spent the next several hours making phone calls because the number he had been given led to another … and another … He finally learned that his daughter was one of the Chi Omega sorority members killed by Ted Bundy.

In the fourth case, the correct city was Denton. The phone number, too, was incorrect. It took two hours and many phone calls for the father to learn that his son, a student at a university in Denton, had been killed.

Gather Significant Data

All too often, emergency physicians on call do not know the person who has died or his or her family members. They meet them for the first time when giving them a death notification.

It is sometimes difficult to establish identity when a person is brought into the hospital emergency department or is taken directly to the medical examiner's office. The notifier must try to balance the need for a timely notification with obtaining accurate details to include in the death notification. In the cases described above, the deaths occurred in communities away from the homes of the surviving family members. In all four cases, the agency responsible for investigating the death notified the law enforcement agency where the family lived and asked them to notify the family in person. This is sometimes called a locate-and-notify mission. This procedure is significantly preferable to notification by phone, but in the above cases, not enough information—or erroneous information—was provided to the notifiers. If the following basic information had been provided, both the notifier and the notified would have been spared unnecessary distress.

The following information should be ascertained before a death notification is made.

- Who died and how the body was identified
- When the death occurred
- Where the death occurred
- Where the body is now
- Any other known information
- A correct phone number the family can call for more information

It is best if notification information is not relayed over law enforcement radio systems. If the family, or friends or neighbors, have a police-band scanner, the family could find out about the death in a shocking way. This could also occur if the family has members who work in the law enforcement or emergency medical professions.

Information in Mass Casualties

The issue of notification becomes even more complex following mass casualty situations such as plane crashes, where only body parts are retrieved. In these cases, fingerprinting, dental records, DNA testing, and radiology may be used, and it often takes weeks or months of investigation before all the victims are identified.

Families want and deserve the truth about every aspect of their loved one's death; and they want that information as immediately as possible after death. Therefore, perhaps the greatest challenge of death notification following mass casualties is gathering complete and accurate information. When family members are encouraged to come to a central location for information, or make their addresses and phone numbers available, this process is simplified.

In these situations, while families wait for information about their individual loved ones, the following information may be obtained from periodic briefings with emergency health care professionals and medical examiners or coroners and shared with the families as a group at a central location or by phone with those who prefer to wait for information at home.

- What happened? Keep the families informed as additional accurate details become available, but also remind them that sometimes inaccurate or incomplete information may be given. If so, it will be corrected as soon as more accurate information is available.
- Where are the injured and the deceased being taken as they are discovered?
- Who is in charge of what?
- What should the waiting families do now?

As names of those believed to be missing or deceased are identified, this information should be shared with families privately, not announced in public or placed on bulletin board lists (as officials did following the tragedy in the New Orleans area after Hurricane Katrina).

More than one source of identification should be utilized if possible. When the identification of bodies or body parts is difficult, a final forensic identification is usually mandatory.

Information in All Deaths

Even when bodies are not significantly damaged, ideal notification can still be difficult. Some people, especially youths, may have more than one driver's license or other types of age identification in their possession. (Some people carry fake IDs.) The use of witnesses who know the person, photos in purses or billfolds that have names written on the back, and identifying marks on the body are but a few additional means of making the identification. The methods that have been used to determine a body's identification should be written down and passed on to the notifier so they can be shared with the family.

In addition to gathering basic information about the person who has died, it is sometimes possible to obtain information about the family to be notified. Personal items in the deceased's pockets, billfold or purse, or in the deceased's vehicle may help identify the family's faith community, place of employment, physician, or insurance company. Prescription bottle labels usually include the prescribing physician's name. Business cards may also be helpful. Such information can be used to contact the family physician, clergy, employer, or other people who may know if the survivor(s) should be notified with any special considerations. If a surviving family member is in fragile medical condition, trained medical personnel should be nearby when the death notification is made. This could save a life.

Plan Who Will Assist in the Death Notification

Consider the Family's Needs

Once all necessary information has been gathered, the next question is who will do the notifying. Selection of the most appropriate notifier(s) is as important as the content of the notification message itself. The one(s) who have "always done it" are not necessarily the best choice. (Notifier selection is addressed more fully in Chapter 3.)

It is preferable to notify in teams of at least two people. This allows better handling of situations where an emergency medical need arises or where children, elderly, or disabled people need special attention.

Notifiers who can be responsive to the unique characteristics of the surviving family can be enormously helpful. If the family's minister, priest, rabbi, imam, or other faith leader can be identified and notified, he or she may be able to assist. If not, hospital or law enforcement chaplains of the family's faith, if this is known, may assist to ensure that the situation is handled in a spiritually sensitive manner. Peoples' spiritual beliefs and practices may be among their greatest sources of resilience, and appropriate rituals that hold meaning for them can be extremely important. Faith leaders who talk too much, however, or who over-spiritualize the death in such a way that grievers are not allowed to mourn, can do more harm than good. So can faith leaders who begin to pray before exploring the family's wishes, or who offer rituals not in keeping with the beliefs and practices of the family. Most hospital chaplains and many law enforcement chaplains are trained to be spiritually sensitive to those of all faiths or no specific faith.

It is recommended that one of the members of the death notification team be a person who was present at the death, so that questions can be answered accurately. This will usually be a doctor or nurse if the death occurred at the hospital, or a law enforcement officer or paramedic if it occurred at the scene of an accident or a crime. In the case of a mass tragedy, the medical examiner is often the person who will have positively identified the victim. He or she would therefore be the one best qualified to answer questions.

A nurse or a social worker may also serve as a notification team member. Law enforcement agencies often use their victim advocates to assist with notifications.

It is ideal if one of the notifiers is trained in dealing with medical emergencies in case of adverse reactions by one of the people notified. In some jurisdictions, law enforcement agencies routinely have emergency medical technicians or paramedics standing by when they notify. The ambulance is stopped a few blocks away rather than directly in front of the family's home or wherever the notification is to take place.

Some have found it beneficial if one of the notifying team is a female. Family members may be more comfortable expressing their vulnerable emotions in the presence of a female rather than a team of males.

Consider the Notifiers' Needs

Notifying in teams of at least two also allows the notifiers to talk together about their own reactions to the death before they deliver the notification (Lord 1997). Death notifications may be especially difficult when a notifier shares similar characteristics with the family to be notified. For example, a notifier who is the father of a teenager notifying a family of their teenager's death may find that death notification especially difficult. Talking about fears and anxieties about the notification beforehand can help to clear the mind so that all attention can be placed on the family. It also offers opportunity for the team to decide who will handle various aspects of the death notification. Being honest about personal emotional reactions is evidence of strength, not of weakness.

One law enforcement officer tells of working with his partner to pull a small boy from a lake after he had drowned. The mother was with her boyfriend in a nearby van, unaware of the child's whereabouts or of efforts to save the child, when they located her and told her of his death. The officers, both fathers, were extremely angry about what had happened and knew they had to talk about it before attempting to notify the child's father. Only then could they move beyond their own reactions and focus fully on the child's father and his needs.

Special Circumstances

Large Groups

If a large group is to be notified, several notifiers may be needed. In some cases, it can simplify the process to inform the entire group at one time. But that is not always the best plan.

For example, a young couple was killed in a car crash. They had been on their way to a family reunion picnic. The large extended family at the picnic included children and elderly persons, some who were in fragile health. A team of six notifiers made the death notification. One notifier approached a family member and asked who were the direct next of kin. These individuals were taken aside and notified privately of the couple's death. Those who now knew of the death gave the notifiers their ideas on how best to tell the others. They decided that various notification team members would inform different age groups.

Another difficult situation arises when several people from different families die in one incident, for example, a car crash involving two or three couples. In such cases, every effort should be made to notify all the immediate families at about the same time. This may avoid one family calling the others and notifying them by phone, thus creating another potential emergency and the likelihood that some families will be upset because they were notified later than others. Given the widespread use of cell phones, text messaging, and the capability of many cell phones to record images, it is more likely than ever before that family or friends who happen upon the scene, or who are notified first, may instantly pass on the information to family and friends.

Line of Duty Deaths

Many law enforcement agencies now have procedures in place for personal notification when an officer is killed in the line of duty, thanks to the efforts of a group called Concerns of Police Survivors (COPS). Far too many departments, however, are still unprepared to deliver death notifications in person to their own law enforcement families.

Some widows and widowers of deceased officers have said that the highest-ranking officer (the chief of police or the sheriff) should make the death notification in person, and that a close colleague of the dead officer (the partner, if possible) accompany as the second notifier.

In order to be as responsive as possible, crisis-responding groups such as police, firefighters, and ambulance personnel could provide in writing his or her death notification wishes when employment begins and revise the document when changes are desired. A sample form is given on the following pages.

Death Notification Information Form

[Name of agency]_____ is committed to providing timely, sensitive notification to families in the event of an emergency. To fulfill this important obligation, it is essential that we have current contact information. Please complete this form and return it to [agency contact]_____

_____

I. Employee's Name:_____
Local address and phone numbers:_____

_____

_____

II. In the event of my injury or death, the first person to be contacted is:
Name: _____
Address:_____
Phone Numbers: _____
I prefer that this person by notified by (name): _____
I prefer that the notifier make the contact:
_____ personally
_____ by phone
_____ other

Does this person have any medical conditions that might be exacerbated by stress? ____ Yes ____No
If yes, please explain:_____

_____

Who is this person's primary care physician?
Name: _____
Phone Number:_____

III. If unable to locate this person within the following amount of time
_____, please notify the following second preference:
Name: _____
Address:_____
Phone Numbers: _____
I prefer that this person by notified by (name): _____
I prefer that the notifier make the contact:
_____ personally
_____ by phone
_____ other
Does this person have any medical conditions that might be exacerbated
by stress? ____ Yes ____ No
If yes, please explain:_____
_____

Who is this person's primary care physician?
Name: _____
Phone Number:_____

IV. In addition, please contact my pastor, priest, rabbi, imam, or
_____
(Circle one title if appropriate, or fill in your preference.)
Name: _____
Address:_____
Phone Number:_____

V. Unless an autopsy is required, my body may be released
to the following funeral home:
Name of funeral home: _____
Phone Numbers: _____

VI. Is there anything else you wish the notifier(s) to know?
_____

Notifications of deaths that occur in the line of duty are complex because the notifying officers, particularly if one of them is the partner, are also grieving. The notifier may try to compartmentalize his or her grief in an effort to be stoic or strong for the surviving spouse. This is rarely, if ever, helpful because it isolates the spouse, making her or him feel alone when comfort and understanding are most needed (Sawyer 1988). In addition, the department may become overly protective and make too many of the decisions and arrangements without consulting the family. This isolates the surviving spouse even further and enhances alienation from those he or she is counting on for support.

Military Deaths

Many of the same issues surround military deaths. Fortunately, the days of yellow, black-edged telegram deliveries are long gone, and policies have been put in place for all branches of the military to deliver notifications personally. Stilted formal language has been replaced with warmer communication styles, but it sometimes takes generations for old styles to change.

Army Reserve Major Alvin Miller remembers that in 1984 he was told to report to his commanding officer, who verified his name and then unceremoniously handed him a piece of paper that said his twelve-year-old brother had been fatally shot back home. "I didn't like the way I was notified," he said. "There was no chaplain, nobody to comfort me or give me hope" (Davis 2003). That episode changed his life. Miller later went to seminary (but was called back to active duty in 2002), and is now serving as chaplain and death notifier at Fort Stewart, Georgia. The revised policy of the U.S. Army is that a notification officer of equal or higher rank than the soldier killed, or than the soldier to be notified, is to deliver the news in person, usually within four hours.

The camaraderie of the military is not unlike that of law enforcement. Similar dangers of inappropriate attempts at protecting survivors can occur. The military, too, sometimes makes decisions surrounding the death of one of its own without gathering as much family opinion as it should, although in recent years many military families report feeling well cared for by those assigned to help them.

Plan the Most Appropriate Physical Setting

Consider each family's unique needs in determining the best physical setting for delivering the crucial information.

Hospice-centered Deaths

Hospice workers usually have some time to prepare the family for the death. They often choose a room other than where the dying patient is lying to say to the family, "It could be weeks, but I suspect it will be days," or, "It could be days, but I suspect it will be hours." These sentences have the potential for more impact than the actual death pronouncement. The benefit of using them is that they give those who wish to be present at the death time to do so. The death itself will be obvious to those present when the person dies. A physician's or coroner's official pronouncement of death will take some time, however.

How to tell those not present is a decision to be made jointly by the family members and the hospice nurse, social worker, or chaplain. Some will need personal notifications at their own homes, some may be called to come to the home or institutional hospice to be told, and some may be distant enough to receive phone notification.

Hospice nurses tend to be highly skilled at cleaning the body and bed linens, removing medical equipment, body fluids, and medications, and making the room attractive for those who choose to view the body before it is taken to the funeral home. Sometimes this includes dimming the lighting and playing soft music. Comfortable chairs need to be available for those who wish to sit for awhile.

Deaths in Hospitals, Nursing Homes, or Other Care Institutions

If the death comes in the hospital or other institutional setting outside the presence of family members, several options may be considered. Some institutions send the family to the chapel before making the notification, but many families have said that this arrangement creates too much anxiety. When asked to go to the chapel, the family members immediately know that their loved one is dead. While well intentioned as a place to offer spiritual support and privacy, another less emotionally laden place is preferable. People generally want to choose when, or if, they will spend time in a chapel. Because most institutional chapels are Judeo-Christian oriented, they are particularly inappropriate for those of other faiths or of no specific faith.

When the dead or dying person is brought to the emergency department of the hospital before the family arrives, ambulance personnel or the hospital staff member taking the call from ambulance personnel should alert a social worker or chaplain about when the family is expected to arrive (Kaul 2001). This allows a compassionate professional to greet the family at the door. If this is not possible, the front desk can be alerted to expect them and to call the social worker or chaplain when they arrive.

If the family is already at the hospital when the death becomes imminent or has already occurred, a nurse should alert the social worker or chaplain.

The family should be accompanied, not sent alone, to a room that is private, comfortably furnished, well lighted (with windows if possible), and equipped with tissues, a bathroom, a pitcher of water, and cups (Parrish et al. 1987). A sofa in the room is useful in the event someone feels faint or needs to lie down. Most people have cell phones today, but survivors say that a phone that can be used without incurring additional charges is very helpful. Sometimes cell phones don't work well within a hospital, are not allowed in the hospital, or batteries may be low, so a land phone is preferable.

While waiting for the physician to come, in order either to update the family on the patient's status (or in some cases to deliver the death notification), the social worker or chaplain may ask the family what they have already been told about the condition of the patient. This is a good opportunity to discern any cultural or spiritual issues that may relate to the situation. Such information can then be relayed to the physician before he or she enters the room. This brief discussion with the social worker or chaplain may help the physician transition from the role of healer to the role of notifier (Kaul 2001). If small children are with the family, one of the notification team may ask parents if the children might be taken to a nearby play area. Older children, however, unless they are particularly vulnerable—perhaps because of mental or emotional disabilities— should usually remain with their parents. More information about notifying children is presented later in this chapter.

Notifications at the Home or at the Scene of a Death

If the notifier is a law enforcement officer, a representative of the military, a chaplain, or a medical examiner or coroner, and the notification is to be given at the family's home, the notifiers will have little control over the setting other than to be sure they have the correct address.

In a situation such as a vehicular crash, the family may be at the scene along with bystanders. Notifiers will need to locate the nearest family members and take them aside to a private place, perhaps inside a patrol vehicle.

Deaths Resulting from Mass Tragedies

Arranging a setting for death notifications following mass tragedies requires complex planning. They are complicated because of media attention and because not all families will be able to receive personal notifications.

Strategizing ahead of time is well worth the effort. If each agency or program's responsibility in responding to a mass tragedy is spelled out ahead of time in a memorandum of understanding (MOU), everything will progress much more smoothly.

Community preplanning should include designating several sites that can function as family care centers or family assistance centers so that, when tragedy happens, a facility near the scene will be available and ready. These centers can be churches, schools, office buildings, or any other easily accessible place that is not difficult to locate.

Some communities have locally funded centers and programs standing ready in the case of a community disaster. In addition to serving as care sites when a crisis occurs, they also offer a place for crisis response training, for trauma grief counseling, and for housing resources on how to serve culturally diverse families and on other types of information and referral services that ensure that the community is ready to provide professional services immediately whenever needed. One example of such a center is the Alachua County Crisis Center in Gainesville, Florida. For more information about this program, go to http://www.alachuacounty.us/government/depts/css/crisis/.

Soon after a large-scale community tragedy, a designated federal agency will take charge. If the crisis involves criminal activity or suspected criminal activity, the FBI will take charge. If it is an accidental transportation disaster, such as a plane crash or railway disaster, the National Transportation Safety Board (NTSB) will take charge. If the so-called accident is suspected to relate to criminal activity, the NTSB and the FBI will work together. The Federal Emergency Management Agency (FEMA) or the Red Cross will take charge of most other large-scale disasters. Any of these federal agencies will be glad to know that the community already has assistance plans in place so that they can work together on all aspects of the community response once their representatives arrive, including death notifications.

In any crisis, the phone number(s) of the designated center (or centers) should be made public as soon as possible. Media should be urged to request that only those who think an immediate family member may be involved in the tragedy use those phone numbers. Families should be asked to designate only one family member to serve as the contact person for the entire family. This avoids unnecessary incoming and outgoing calls. It is also crucial that survivors in, or near, the tragedy scene immediately notify their own family members of their safety so that their families will not tie up centers' phones. This includes rescue workers.

When concerned family members contact the center, they should be asked if they wish to remain at home to await information or if they wish to come to the center. Their wishes should be carefully noted and followed. Ideally, communities will have notification teams and procedures in place so that personal status notifications can be made to those who wish to remain at home. Law enforcement officers or chaplains who have been trained in death notification may make the death notifications in person.   But if teams of volunteers from the local chapter of the American Red Cross, or groups of hospital chaplains or mental health professionals are trained ahead of time for this task, then law enforcement officers may be freed for other duties.

Families who choose to come to the center will need to provide identification before being admitted. This prevents unwanted media representatives and other concerned but untrained people from accessing families. Family members may also be asked to bring photos, dental records, and other data to help identify their loved one(s).

A room similar to that previously described, but larger—and with computers and more phones—should be available for the families to use. If the room is large enough, it should have several televisions because families will be eager to hear any updates the media may be providing and may want different groups watching different networks. The room should include bulletin boards for messages. Preplanning should also include enlistment of restaurants, charities, and faith communities to provide food for the families at the center. Likewise, hotels that will donate rooms and other services to the involved families may be enlisted ahead of time.

When a loved one's body is identified, the family should be told in a private, comfortable room if they are at the center. Or they should be personally notified in their own home if they are not at the center.

For more information on mass community tragedy response, see *Mental Health Response to Mass Violence and Terrorism* published by the U.S. Department of Health and Human Services and the U.S. Department of Justice. The publication is available at www.samhsa.gov/trauma/index.aspx .

Adjust for Complicating Factors

Even with the best plans, death notifications can become complicated. For example, the family to be notified at their home may not be there. In this case, the notifier may be able to locate a neighbor who is at home, and ask how to locate the family about an emergency. It is best not to tell neighbors about the death because the immediate family may become upset that the neighbor was told first. In addition, this puts the neighbor in the difficult position of becoming the notifier with only second-hand information.

If the family member is at work and his or her place of employment can be identified, the notifier may go there, ask for the supervisor, and request that the employee be brought to a private room. As with a neighbor, the supervisor should not be told of the death first—unless access to the employee is otherwise denied. When the only alternative is a phone call, tell the supervisor and ask him or her to personally notify the employee, preferably with someone in the workplace who is a close friend.

If only one immediate family member, perhaps a parent, is at home and the other parent—or a noncustodial parent—is not there, it is usually best to notify the one who is at home. Then ask if he or she would like to go along to notify other immediate or otherwise vulnerable relatives or friends, who might be overly traumatized by a phone message.

Consider Clothing and Other Personal Property Issues

In addition to planning who will make the death notification and where it is planned to take place, careful decisions about clothing and personal property help ensure a compassionate and competent process.

If the notifier's uniform has become soiled by the deceased's body fluids or anything else, he or she should put on a clean jacket or uniform before delivering the death notification. Clean, well pressed attire projects order that can be calming.

In Medical Examiner cases, clothing, jewelry, billfold, purse, or other personal items of the deceased will need to go with the body. Following other deaths, it is still not a good idea to take these items to the death notification. Most families need time to prepare psychologically before receiving these things. It is preferable that the hospital social worker or chaplain store these items until the family is ready to receive them. Another alternative is to send them with the deceased to the funeral home, but the more these items change hands the greater the chance that something will get lost.

Notify Without Memorizing

Introduce Yourself

The warmth of the notifier serves as something of a buffer to the information to be delivered. For this reason, notifiers should begin the process by introducing themselves to the family if they have not met before. Introductions need only to include the name and basic credential of the notifier. If a notifier is not in a uniform that speaks for his or her role, it is a good idea to follow the introduction by presenting an identification card or a business card.

This introduction should not be formal. Unfortunately, some law enforcement protocols for death notification are still based on the old military model. One such model requires that

> ...the (CNO) Casualty Notification Officer to go to the home of the NOK (next of kin) in Class A uniform and deliver the following memorized statement: "I am Captain Sam Robinson from Company A, 2nd Battalion, 21st Infantry, Fort Bragg, North Carolina. The Secretary of the Army has asked me to express his deep regret that your son, Robert, was killed in action on March 10, 1996. [State circumstances provided by Casualty Area Command.] The Secretary extends his deepest sympathy to you and your family in this tragic loss." (U.S. Army 1994)

The military now acknowledges that this formal style is not helpful to families and it has relaxed its procedures to allow more flexibility and warmth in death notifications. In the army, both Casualty Notification Officers and Casualty Assistance Officers, who are the ones to follow up with families after the notification, attend a forty-hour training program to prepare them for their duties.

If the death notification is taking place at the home of the surviving family, the notifier should ask to come in. Notifiers, particularly law enforcement notifiers, must be aware that some families will have had enough negative experiences with law enforcement that they will be reluctant to allow entrance. Spiritual and cultural sensitivities play a role, too, in that Muslim women who cover their hair will not want to allow a male into their home with their hair uncovered or if a male family member is not there. In these cases, the notifier may need to wait until it is acceptable to enter.

If able to enter the home and in institutional settings, the notifier should ask everyone to sit down. When they are seated, the notifier should sit down with them. The purpose of getting the family seated is to prevent falls if someone faints or experiences a sudden blood pressure change. Sometimes, out of immense distress, a family member may attempt to assault or hit the notifier. Being seated makes this more difficult.

This practice, while ideal, may have to be abandoned if the family has already come outside or does not want the notifier to enter the home. Likewise, it cannot be achieved when the family has come to a death scene away from the home. In these cases, it is worth trying to get them to sit on the grass or curb. If they refuse, then the death notification will have to be conducted with everyone standing.

Identify the Immediate Family

In hospital deaths, the social worker or chaplain hopefully will have already met the family, identified the nearest next of kin, and offered to take small children to a play area. In other cases, it will fall to the notifier to determine who is who. The simplest way to do this is to use the deceased's name and the assumed relationship to the deceased following the notifier's introduction. For example, "Are you the parents of [name]?" This question should be in the present tense: "Are you the parents…?" rather than "Were you the parents…?"

Next, the notifier must quickly assess whether to tell everyone together which may be preferable if all are adults, or to separate the group. If small children, elderly, or otherwise vulnerable people are present, it may be best to ask primary adult next of kin if you can move to a private area. Notifying all adults at the same time simplifies things later, when family members compare notes about what was said. Several death notifications leave open the possibility of more misunderstanding.

Once any necessary separating is complete, the preparation statement may be given.

Deliver the Preparation Statement

Before coming to the heart of the death notification, the notifier should briefly review what happened. This information should not include every detail, because it must be short. The family will already be anxious, so they cannot mentally process an overly detailed account (McEwen 2000). The brief lead-in, however, gives the family an opportunity to begin to prepare for the death announcement itself.

If the death was sudden and unanticipated, it may be best for the preparation statement to begin with the notifier's first knowledge of the person who died. Basically, it should include both the circumstances surrounding the incident that led to the death and the basic treatment attempted. In planning how to communicate this information, it is best to stick with the bare facts. It is also important not to guess or fill in information not yet known (Stewart 1999).

The preparation statement a physician makes to a family at the hospital might be: "Your daughter Jane was brought in at ten-thirty with very severe injuries to her chest and neck. She was unconscious. We attempted resuscitation for twenty minutes, doing everything we could to revive her."

The preparation statement made at a family's home by a law enforcement officer might be something like the following. "About nine p.m. I received a call to go to Oak Street, where there had been a car crash. I could tell it was serious, and when I went up closer, I could see that your son Jason was unconscious and was being treated by paramedics. They attempted resuscitation for twenty minutes and did everything they could to revive him."

If family members arrive at the scene of an auto accident, the officer can tell them briefly what he or she knows about the crash. If the injured family member is still alive, it helps to explain what emergency medical personnel are doing, for example, "The crash occurred about twenty-five minutes ago. Emergency Medical Services arrived about fifteen minutes ago and they're now treating the people in the vehicle(s)."

Although it is important not to include much detail in these preparatory statements, family may well want detail after the death statement has been made. For this reason, written notes with more detail give the notifier information that may be needed to answer questions, whenever they may be asked. Unable to comprehend complex information at the moment of death notification, many family members want details after the initial waves of grief have subsided a little. Others may ask for it weeks or months later. Some never do.

Make The Core Death Notification Statement

Experiential Exercises

The following examples illustrate the long-lasting effect of death notifications in which those responsible did not take the time or make the effort to determine the most compassionate way to locate and notify loved ones. Read them, and answer the question that follows.

April 2, 1996, was a day that began like most other spring days. My two-year-old grandson had spent the night with me so that my daughter (his mom) could go out with her sister and some friends to celebrate her twenty-second birthday. I took my grandson to work with me that morning, and we came home at noon for lunch. My neighbor came over and handed me a death notice from the Philadelphia Police Department. It told me to contact the Accident Investigation Division in relation to my daughters.

There is no way for me to describe the absolute terror I felt in reading that notice. The thought that two of my children were gone, and that my grandson had been left without a mother, was more than I could handle. The details after those first moments are a blur to me. I only know that to this day I am appalled by the absolute insensitivity of the officer who left that notice.

I finally did discover that the daughter who was the mother of my grandson had been killed in the auto accident. Her sister and their friends survived.

I share this story with the hope that all officers responsible for delivering a death notice will treat that responsibility with the same level of dignity and respect that they would use to tell their own husband or wife that their child has been killed.

Helen Wiegand – Philadelphia, PA

In California, a young woman and her fiancé went out with friends the evening before his birthday. She had sprained her ankle several days before and decided to go home early. About 12:30 a.m., she was awakened by a phone call from her fiancé's friend, obviously in shock. He told her they had been involved in an accident. Then he hung up.

The young woman called hospital after hospital and finally found the one that told her that her fiancé was dead. All she remembers is screaming and running through the house until a neighbor found her, incoherent.

Two young couples went out against their parents' wishes and were engaged in street racing when the car crashed, killing one of the girls. The other girl was not injured and immediately called her own mother, who rushed to the scene. The mother thought she could notify the dead girl's mother by cell phone, but after the phone rang, she couldn't do it. Seconds later, a police officer got on the phone and said the words the mother of the dead girl would never forget: "I cannot tell you exactly who it is, but I do have a deceased female at the scene."

Based on what you have learned so far, how might these three notifications have been conducted more appropriately? The point, obviously, is that collection of accurate basic information and personal notification are both crucial and ideal, but compassion demands that adjustments sometimes be made. Telephone notifications can produce disastrous reactions, especially when a family member is home alone.

In Fort Worth, Texas, an employee of the medical examiner's office called a home for dental records of a young man who had been burned to death, assuming that the family had been notified. They had not been. The young man's elderly father was home alone when he answered the phone. He suffered a heart attack and died. A funeral for both the father and son were held simultaneously two days later (Sanders and Stavish 1995).

Move into the Core Message

The actual death notification message following the preparation statement should be simple and direct, and delivered with warmth and compassion (Lord 1997; Stewart 1999).

Linking the preparation statement to the death notification with another brief statement will give them a few more seconds to prepare for it. "I'm afraid the information I have for you is not good" is a good example. After a slight pause to let them attempt to assimilate the statement, the death notification should be given.

That sentence should include the deceased's name. "John has suffered irreparable injury, and even though every attempt was made to save his life, those efforts were not successful ... and he has died."

If the cause of death is suicide, the words "took his own life" are better than "completed a suicide" or "committed a successful suicide." The statement might be, "Bob apparently injured himself very severely by [method]. Even though every effort to save his life was attempted, those efforts were not successful. He took his own life, and he has died."

The word "died" is very important and should be used several times. Phrases like fatally injured, expired, passed away, passed on, or we've lost [name] can cause confusion in loved ones who are not thinking clearly because of the shock of the situation. It is important to avoid enabling family members to misconstrue the message, as they desperately hope that their loved one is still alive.

Express Empathy

"I'm so sorry" may seem like a trivial follow-up comment, but it isn't trivial. After just relaying devastating information, this statement, which expresses an emotional reaction, is a welcome change from the hard facts. It communicates to the family that the notifier is a warm, caring individual. Furthermore, it subtly invites family members to react emotionally as well. It can cut through false perceptions that they need to be strong or that they should not show their feelings. It allows the genuine ventilating of emotion that comes naturally for most people.

Notifiers, too, feel better about themselves after they have let the family know they care about the suffering the death information has brought.

Listen

Allow Survivors Time to Absorb the Information and React

After delivering the actual death announcement, no more words are necessary until a family member is able to speak. The family's silence, or agonizing expressions of emotional reaction, may seem to last forever, but this is not the case. This is sacred time, and it is important not to clutter it with words that won't be heard or understood.

It is not helpful to try to say wise or comforting things to the family during this time of silence or emotional reaction. It takes concentration and practice to learn to be comfortable with silence.

Notifiers must understand that a vastly wide range of emotional reactions is perfectly natural (Lord 1997, 2006). Some people will react with a primitive fight-or-flight response, much like that of a frightened animal. Those whose basic reaction to stress is to become aggressive may curse, blame the notifier, or hit someone or something.

Those whose basic reaction to stress is to flee may retreat to another room, run outside, or faint.

Some may become behaviorally frozen. They may simply stare wide-eyed, incapable of doing or saying anything.

Some may begin immediately to cry, moan, or wail.

None of these reactions are abnormal or unnatural. Just as there are many different kinds of people, there are many acceptable ways of reacting following a death notification. Because emotional reactions are not planned, they simply happen. People cry, for example, because they need to cry.

Once these reactions are understood as natural, it becomes easier for the notifier to cope with them and simply let them run their course. A wise notifier allows family members to have their reactions without trying to say something to stop or even shorten them.

Some notifiers believe they should be "strong" during a death notification. This is a false belief. The family does need calm, respectful support, but people also appreciate genuine emotional reaction. If the notifier's eyes well up a bit, no harm is done. It is simply honest, caring communication, and it can mean a lot to family members.

One elderly woman spoke of the notification of the death of her husband more than thirty years ago. The notifying officer knelt down beside her, took her hand and told her as gently as he could. He told her how sorry he was. She was very appreciative of the fact that he told her as a person, not as if in a role he was required to fulfill. To this day, she holds him in highest esteem and, in fact, has generalized that respect to all law enforcement officers.

If a family member begins to assault someone, including the notifier, it works best to try to gently hold him or her in a way that feels supportive and yet prevents further attack. A person who feels unduly controlled or restrained may fight even harder. With gentle support, most people calm down. Often they even apologize.

Occasionally, someone will go into shock, which is a sudden decrease in the function of vital processes of the body. Symptoms include feeling faint (a temporary loss of blood to the brain), pale skin, rapid but weak pulse, rapid and shallow breathing, sweating on the palms or other body parts, and nausea or vomiting. If someone develops these symptoms, the person should be guided or carried to a place where he or she can lie down. The head should be lowered and the feet elevated to assist blood flow to the brain. One of the death notification team should keep the person warm, and monitor breathing and pulse. Another can call for medical assistance so that medical consequences can be either ruled out or treated.

Address Special Needs of Children

Because older children and adolescents generally handle death notifications in ways similar to adults, they can usually be present for the adult death notification. Every effort should be made to notify small children separately, however. Witnessing the emotional collapse of their caretakers can be as upsetting to children as the death itself.

Before she died at the age of ninety-six, Sarah "Sally" Carver still recalled with gratitude how a sheriff's deputy notified her, as a young woman in her early thirties, that her husband had been killed. Her husband had been a widower who brought nine children into the marriage, and Sally and her husband had had several more of their own. When the deputy arrived at the family farm, he led Sally away from the house and children, and told her of the death. The children could not overhear the information or witness her reaction. His thoughtfulness and kindness stayed with Sally for the rest of her life.

Once the adults have been notified, the notifier can discuss with them how to tell the small children. In some cases, one of the adults will want to do it. In other cases, they will want the notifier to tell the children, or to tell them together.

Regardless of who tells them, children deserve to be told the truth. The less they are told, the more they will have to fill in the gaps from what they overhear, which can lead to significant misconceptions of the truth.

One boy overheard only that his mother had tripped over a stool and died. The boy had left the stool in the middle of the room. He suffered guilt and depression for years until he was finally told that his mother had had a heart attack and that the stool had nothing to do with her death.

A ten-year-old girl was on a visitation with her divorced father when he told her that she would not be going back home to her mother. The only explanation the father gave was that her mother had gone to be with her brother, who had died earlier. The girl chose not to believe the story but had no facts with which to replace it. No one talked about her mother's death. Her mother's pictures were removed from sight and, apparently, the father never looked back. When the girl became twenty-eight years old, she sought counseling for severe depression. Her therapist encouraged her to find out what had happened. She learned that the man her mother was dating had murdered her. The daughter would have been far better able to accommodate to her mother's death, tragic as it was, if she had been told the truth rather then left in the dark all those years.

If a notifier goes to the home to make a death notification, and only children or adolescents are home, the notifier should try to ascertain when adults will return, and leave. Children and adolescents will be extremely upset by the information they hear, and they will feel even more helpless with no adult caretakers to support them. They will then find themselves in the position of having to notify their own caretakers. In addition, parents and spouses are likely to be very upset if adolescent siblings or other relatives are notified first.

Several years ago, in Miami, parents had realized their teenage son was not home and went out looking for him, leaving his teenage sister home in bed. While they were gone, an officer came to the home. The girl answered the door and was told that her brother was dead. The officer left, and she ran to her parents' bedroom. They were gone and she didn't know where they were. The girl suffered severe emotional distress for years.

In an Oregon case, a family realized that a crash had occurred down the road from them, so they sent their teenage son to see what had happened. As he approached the scene, he recognized his brother's car. An officer asked the boy who he was. When he gave his name, the officer handed him his brother's billfold. The boy then asked if his brother had been taken to the hospital. The officer responded, "No, he's been taken to the mortuary." The brother had to drive back home alone and tell his parents that they were to go to mortuary to identify his brother. No one from the sheriff's department ever went to the parents' home, apparently believing that the family had been appropriately notified. The brother required intensive counseling for an extended period of time.

Sometimes, adult family members do not speak English and routinely use their children to translate. In such a situation a notifier still should never ask a child or adolescent to translate a death notification message to non-English-speaking adults. The child will be traumatized by what he or she is hearing and then will have to face the burden of becoming the notifier for his own family. This is too much to ask of a child or adolescent. One alternative is for the notifier to ask the English-speaking child to provide the location of a nearby relative or friend who understands both English and the family's language. This adult can be notified and if all goes well, that adult can then return with the notifier to tell the immediate family. Of course the ideal scenario is for notifying agencies to have lists of trained people representing major languages spoken within a community. These people can assist on a death notification team as needed.

Answer Questions Honestly

After the initial emotional reaction has run its course, it is difficult to say what will happen next. In most cases, a family member will ask a question. Therefore, it is important that notifiers remain present after the death notification is made. This is true for notifications to adults and to small children.

Notifiers should attempt to answer every question honestly and briefly. Given the strong emotions they are experiencing, survivors are unlikely to absorb complex details (Lord 2006). In the days or weeks after the initial notification, survivors may contact the notifier to request further information about the events that led to the death. In all question sessions, honesty is crucial.

A dishonest answer, perhaps later revealed in court proceedings or other venues, can cause irreparable harm. Families feel betrayed if they specifically ask for important information at the time of the death notification, and then learn later, from a court proceeding or from an autopsy report, that the information they received from their notifiers was either inaccurate or dishonest. The survivors may wonder what else they were not told. Such a situation does more than destroy the credibility of the notifier. It shakes the survivors' faith in the entire institution that the notifier represents.

If the notifier does not know the answer to a question, he or she should say so. The notifier can then offer to get the answer for the family or find out how the family can get it themselves. If the family wants to obtain it themselves, the notifier should write down how to get that information. Family members are likely to have trouble remembering what they were told.

As notifiers give honest answers, they should try not to volunteer information that places responsibility on the deceased for what happened (with the exception of suicide). This is important even when the deceased seems to be at fault. Following a trauma-related death, family members may ask, for example, if alcohol or other drugs were involved. Toxicology reports will not be available immediately, but if there is evidence such as bottles, cans, or drug paraphernalia at the death scene, notifiers should tell the truth.

Some may ask if the deceased suffered at the end. Notifiers should never fabricate an answer to this question, but should answer it minimally without distorting the truth. If the notifier witnessed the death and there was no obvious suffering, the family will be comforted by this information. If suffering was observed, an answer might be, "It is never possible to know for sure because the body sometimes reacts involuntarily even when a person is unconscious. What I saw, however, was ____." Such a statement should be short. If the notifier is a medical professional, he or she can tell the family what, if any, medications were administered to decrease pain. Assurances such as "Most people who are severely injured do not remember the direct assault and do not feel pain for some time," and "Death occurs very quickly after the rupture of the aorta" are almost always true statements.

Avoid Euphemisms

As conversation continues, it is best to repeat the words dead or died several more times to help family members more fully absorb the death. Continue to use their loved one's name, and avoid words like body, corpse, remains, the deceased, or worse, the impersonal "it." For example, you might say, "Johnny will probably be at the medical examiner's office for a couple of days." The use of the person's name conveys dignity to the person who died and demonstrates the notifier's respect for the deceased as well as for the survivors.

Lapses in the conversation can create the temptation to speak unnecessary platitudes that are usually resented more than they are appreciated. It is natural for notifiers to want to do or say something that will make the family feel better. But silence on the part of the notifier is preferred because it is impossible for them to feel better when they have just been told that a loved one has died. Instead of making inappropriate statements, it is usually better to simply honor the person's natural emotional reaction to the news of the death. Less is more in these situations. Rather than trying to cheer up the family, let silence reign for a bit and then use some of the statements suggested below.

What Can Be Said

The following is a short list of statements that survivors surveyed have said are helpful. Reasons why they are considered helpful are given in parentheses (Lord 1997).

- I'm so sorry. (Simple, direct, and validating.)
- This is harder than most people think. (Validates their reactions and encourages them to seek support.)
- Most people who have gone through this react similarly to you. (Validates reactions.)
- People can experience many different feelings at the same time. (Validates the flood of different and sometimes conflicting reactions that people experience.)
- This is one of the most difficult times in your life.
- Is there anything you would like to tell me or ask me?
- Is there anyone I can contact for you before I leave?
- [When ready to leave] I'll check back with you tomorrow to see

how you're doing. If there's anything else I can do for you before then, please let me know. Here's my phone number [or business card]. (Validates the significance of the loss, expresses concern, and introduces an element of control.)

What Should Not Be Said

Here is a long list of inappropriate responses to families that should be avoided (Lord 1997). Clues about why the response is unhelpful are given in parentheses.

- I know how you feel. (You don't.)
- Time heals all wounds. (It doesn't.)
- You need to be strong. (They don't, not after just hearing such upsetting information.)
- You need to take it like a man. (If this means not having, or not showing, emotional reactions, this is not true . . . for either gender.)
- At least you made it out alive. (Many survivors have a great deal of guilt about living when others have died and may be more focused on that guilt than on relief at their own survival.)
- You'll get over this someday. (They will get better, but they are not likely to "get over it.")
- He was just in the wrong place at the wrong time. (Trite)
- You must go on with your life. (They will, the best way they can, but they don't need to be told to do so.)
- He didn't know what hit him. (Unless you're sure.)
- You can always find someone worse off than yourself. (This discounts their honest reaction, and it is not true at the moment.)
- You can't bring him back. (They know that.)
- It's best to remember him the way he was. (This is usually stated when attempting to prevent someone from viewing his or her loved one's body. If they want to see their loved one, don't try to deter them. Instead, do your best to help them do so. There is information on how to facilitate viewing the body below.)
- You don't need to know that. (Yes they do, or they wouldn't have asked.)

- You don't want to see her. (People know what they want and what they can or cannot handle.)
- I can't tell you that. (If you can't answer the question, explain why, and tell the family when they can expect to have an answer.)
- It must have been his/her time. (You do not know this.)
- Someday you'll understand why. (They may never understand why.)
- It was actually a blessing because… (You do not know this.)
- God must have needed her more than you did. (No one fully understands the nature of spiritual reality.)
- God never gives us more than we can handle. (Even if this is true, the family does not need to feel guilty for the difficulty they are experiencing.)
- Only the good die young. (Trite and unproven.)
- You've got to take control of yourself. (No reason.)
- I'm going to make sure this guy gets the death penalty. (Never make promises about the justice system.)
- Now that you know, I need you to come to the station with me to answer some questions. (This points out one reason the homicide detective following through on an investigation should not deliver the death notification.)

One final don't is the word "closure." Not only is this word vastly overused, but also it is unrealistic, especially following sudden deaths such as suicides, homicides, and vehicular crashes. Because of the lack of preparation for the death and the shock of the notification, the death is never forgotten. Family members do get better, but they rarely, if ever, experience full healing or closure.

Give Practical Assistance and Information

After the death message has been given and family's initial emotional reactions have begun to subside, the death notification process is not yet complete. It is equally important to help the family decide what to do next.

It may be necessary for other immediate family members to be personally notified, and a decision will need to be made about who will do that and how it will best be accomplished.

If children are at school, some families choose to wait until the child comes home to tell them what happened. Others feel that their children should be told as soon as possible. In the latter case, the primary caregiver(s) should go to the school and tell them there. This avoids taking a child out of class, and driving them home in the presence of an unstated but obviously serious situation before telling them what has happened. The literature on death notifications at school is limited, but Servaty-Seib, Peterson, and Spang (2003) recommend that the school counselor be told first and, together with the parents, they can decide how to tell the child. The child can then be brought to the counselor's office, which usually offers privacy, comfort, and perceived safety. Informed counselors can support the entire family during the death notification, and may be able to provide ongoing support for the children when in the school setting. For example, a school counselor, aware of what has happened, is in a good position to seek reasonable concessions from the principal and from teachers in regard to absences and homework.

Before leaving the death notification setting, the notifier should offer to make calls to other survivors, who may not require notification in person, but need to know what has happened. These types of survivors may include employers, faith leaders, and close friends. Perhaps it will be helpful to call someone to come and care for small children, elderly family members, or pets. If the family wishes the notifier to make these calls, then the notifier should write down the names of the persons he or she has contacted, and the time call was made. After such a list is delivered, this gives the grieving family members—who can be too stressed to remember details—a way to check who has, and who has not yet been notified.

Grief and trauma reactions come in waves, so it is important to remain with the family long enough for the initial reaction to subside and to assess how much additional help may be needed.

Address Organ/Tissue Donation and Autopsy

When organ or tissue donation is an option, as is often the case following hospital deaths, hospital staff may ask the family if they would like organs to be donated. This is not the death notifier's responsibility, but notifiers need to be educated about organ donation if the family brings it up. The primary deciding medical factor on whether donation is possible is the deceased person's physical condition at the time of death. If the death was sudden and occurred away from a medical facility where the person could not be immediately placed on a ventilator to keep the organs functioning until they could be removed, then organ donation may not be an option.

The person's age is not a factor. Newborns as well as senior citizens can be organ donors.

The secondary major factor in determining the suitability of donation of organs or tissue is, according to the National Institutes of Health (2007), the urgency of need. If the person can be placed on a ventilator, the medical staff will determine acceptability of organs and tissue based on both the donor's general health and the urgency of recipient need.

Notifiers should be prepared to answer the common question "Will donation disfigure the body and interfere with an open casket service?" The answer is no. Answers to other organ donation questions should be referred to donation and transplantation specialists at the hospital.

It is important that the family understand that the team of physicians and staff who tried valiantly to save their loved one's life is separate from the organ donation or transplant teams (National Women's Health Information Center 2007). If this distinction is not made clear, the family may question whether all treatment options to save their loved one were utilized at a time when organs were needed by someone else. Distressed and confused family members who feel powerless about their loved one's death, or impending death, may question whether all possible life-saving treatments were administered. Notifiers should be alert to this possible need for reassurance, and provide written information on the structure of the separation in any given facility.

Organ donation is an area where spiritual sensitivity is crucial. Some Reform Jews and Christians may be open to discussion about organ donation, but most Native Americans, Hindus, Buddhists, Orthodox Jews, Conservative Jews, and Muslims are not likely to consider it. Native Americans usually want their loved ones' bodies to go to the spirit world intact. Some tribes fear that donated body parts might be used in harmful ways. Hindus and many Buddhists believe that the karma of the deceased person accompanies his or her organs, and if organs are removed, the spirit of the deceased may find it more difficult to depart to prepare for the next rebirth. Some, however, may feel that offering part of one's body so that another may live will reap positive karma for them. Wise notifiers will not bring up organ donation with those who are known to avoid it. In some jurisdictions, it has been deemed mandatory to address organ and tissue donation. In these situations, spiritual diversity education is crucial.

When a family's feelings are not known but likely to be culturally against organ or tissue donation, transplant teams can ask the family if they would like a leader of the their faith to discuss it with them. Even then, however, it should be remembered that families don't always share the same values about such matters as their faith's tenets suggest. The immediate family and the transplant team will make the ultimate decision.

When legally required, autopsy is another topic that will require discussion. In most states, autopsy is mandatory when a person dies unattended by a physician (or is attended for less than twenty-four hours), when a crime is suspected, or when the attending physician is uncomfortable attributing cause of death. An autopsy also may be ordered when a public health concern is involved—such as the presence of a contagious disease or when questions are raised about the quality of care given. A coroner holds a political position, so the coroner may or may not be a physician. A medical examiner is always a physician, usually a pathologist. Exactly who makes the decision about mandatory autopsy depends on the jurisdiction.

If an autopsy is determined to be legally mandated, the loved one's body is usually taken to a state-designated medical examiner's office, where a pathologist performs the procedure. A pathologist is a physician specializing in the scientific study of body parts, illnesses, diseases, and causes of death. Medical examiners typically spend a year or more conducting autopsies as part of their professional training after medical school. It is much like a surgical procedure in a hospital. As with organ donation, a body that has been autopsied is left in a state that allows it still to be viewable at an open casket funeral.

When an autopsy is not mandated, the family can still ask the hospital to perform one if they desire it. Notifiers will generally not suggest this, but if the family brings it up they can tell them that it can be done. It sometimes is important to tell the family that hospital pathologists are independent from the physicians who treat patients, and that autopsies, when performed by hospital pathologists, are usually free. If the family prefers, however, a private pathologist can be asked to conduct an autopsy in the funeral home or elsewhere.

In either mandated or requested autopsies, it is the legally recognized next of kin who must sign the autopsy permit.

Mandatory autopsy is upsetting to most families, especially those with religious prohibitions about it. It sometimes helps if the family's spiritual leader conducts the expected rituals over the body before the autopsy begins, or if the faith leader is present during the autopsy.

Hindus prefer to cremate as soon as possible after a death, so both the delay in burial that the autopsy causes and the actual cutting of the body are believed to make transition of the spirit more difficult. Both Hindus and Buddhists feel that proper preparation of the body in safe, serene surroundings is important for transition of the spirit to prepare for rebirth. In Orthodox Judaism, embalming and autopsy are believed to disrupt both simplicity and respect for the body as it begins the natural decomposition process. Reform and some Conservative Jewish families may be more open to autopsy. Muslims do not embalm or cremate and they find autopsy unacceptable unless mandated by law. Violating the modesty requirements of Islam is also very disturbing to Muslims, so during any mandatory autopsy, medical examiners should keep as much of the body covered as possible while each organ is examined.

Discuss Viewing the Body

Viewing the body is an important issue for notifiers because many family members want to see their loved one's body as soon as possible, particularly after a sudden and unanticipated death (Awooner-Renner 1991; Lord 2006). This desire may be strong for those whose religions do not prohibit viewing dead bodies. Unlike anticipated deaths, where family members have the opportunity to deal lovingly with the dying person for some period of time, families whose loved ones have died suddenly had no opportunity to say "I love you," "I'm sorry," "Good-bye," or other essential messages that family members desperately wish they could have communicated (Lord 2006). Thus, they need to say these things the best way they can … after the death.

Viewing after Deaths in Health Care Facilities

Viewing the body in a hospital or other health care setting is not complex, but it is an aspect of death notification that the notifier should be ready to address, in order to ensure a smooth process (Stewart 1999). If the patient dies in his or her own hospital room, some family members may be present at the time of death. Other family members, however, may not be in the room at the time. If the death occurred in surgery or in the emergency department, none of the family is likely to have been present, although more and more emergency departments are allowing family members to be present during life-saving efforts. In these cases, the social worker, chaplain, or nurse should explain what the scene looks like so family members can make an informed decision about going in.

After a death, those who wish to view the body should be given permission to do so after being given a full description of what they can expect to see. Unless a requirement for autopsy disallows it, the body should first be cleaned and covered with a clean sheet or warming blanket, and tubes should be removed, as should items containing body fluids. In some jurisdictions, medical examiners require that the body first be placed in a body bag and then covered with a blanket before the family comes in. Medical equipment used in treatment efforts may remain in the room. These can indicate to the family some of the significant efforts made to save their loved one. If possible, a hand of the deceased can be placed outside the sheet or blanket so it can be touched or held. Softening the lighting can enhance the setting as well.

It is preferable that the loved one be viewed in a room other than the hospital morgue. Those wishing to view the body should be reminded that the body is pale, no longer warm to the touch, and possibly stiffening. While this is obvious to medical personnel, many families are naive about these aspects and may find these body characteristics upsetting if they are not prepared ahead of time. If people, especially parents of children who have died, wish to hold the body, this should be allowed. If there is possible criminality involved, the medical examiner may not permit holding or touching in order to not disturb evidence on the body.

Viewing After Deaths Outside a Health Care Facility

When a person dies outside a hospital and not at home, complications may arise in arranging viewing. Notifiers should work with the medical examiner's office to develop procedures for viewing bodies before the loved one is removed to a funeral home.

In communities where this procedure is well developed, the notifier informs the medical examiner's office as soon as the family requests visitation. The body of the deceased is cleaned and wounds that might be particularly distressing to the family are covered with a clean sheet or towel. When the family members arrive for the viewing, they are told the exact condition of the body, including where wounds are obvious. They are reminded that the body is now pale because blood has settled to the lower parts of the body. After being given this information, the family should again be offered the decision to view or not.

If they still choose to do so, they should be taken to the room where their loved one has been placed. Someone should stand at a distance from the body, available to again briefly explain the condition of the loved one's body, if questions arise. A nearby staff member may also be needed to provide emergency medical care in the event that someone goes into shock or faints.

If family members wish to move closer and touch the body, they should be allowed to do so as long as it will not interfere with any forthcoming examination. In some cases a family member may request to see a wound that has been covered. If they make this request, it is only because they feel the need to do so. The request should be granted and an offer should be made to describe the wound before it is uncovered. Either way, family members who feel the need to see their loved one right away are always grateful when their request can be granted, even in cases where the visitation can be offered only after the autopsy is completed.

Many medical examiners' offices require a person to identify the body even when family members do not want to. Notifiers should be aware that there are means of identification other than a person visually confirming the identity of the body. Such means include a description of tattoos, unique clothing or jewelry the victim is wearing, X-ray or dental records, and viewing only a hand or a foot. Use of these means can meet identification requirements while ensuring that the family's choice not to view the body is honored when at all possible (Schwartz 2003).

A good resource for information about appropriate care of families in a medical examiner's office is the Wendt Center for Loss and Healing, affiliated with the District of Columbia Medical Examiner's Office. For more information, go to www.wendtcenter.org.

Regardless of whether the death notification and/or viewing of the body takes place at the scene of an accident, at the home, at the hospital, or at the medical examiner's office, family members should never be left alone until they have their own sources of personal support with them. If the notifier has phoned other family members, faith leaders, or other requested supportive people, he or she should remain with the family until these persons arrive. If the death notification has been made at the home, and family members have requested to go to the hospital or medical examiner's office to view the body, the notifier should drive them for the viewing. People in a distressed frame of mind do not always drive safely. If other support persons are unavailable, this same notifier should take the family back home or call a cab for them.

Deaths in which Bodies Cannot Easily Be Retrieved

Sometimes, particularly in military deaths and deaths in mass community tragedies, there is no body to view. Family members find this situation particularly devastating, and it can cause them to have difficulty realizing that their loved one is actually dead. It can take months before body parts are collected and identified, and in some cases, no body parts are ever retrieved. When a recovery operation ends before all bodies are recovered, families tend to feel that their loved one is being abandoned.

Family members in these situations may find it meaningful to go to the site of the death. For example, after such disasters as airplane crashes, families may want to go to the area where the plane went down, whether on land or in water. Boating clubs sometimes volunteer to arrange these outings following water disasters. Traveling to the death site may validate the family's need to honor and memorialize their loved one. Sometimes body parts that are not identifiable are placed in a communal casket for burial, and some family members may find it meaningful to attend such burial rituals.

When no remains are recovered, symbolic materials or artifacts may provide some comfort. Following 9/11, many family members were given an urn of ashes from the scene. The brother of a man missing from the World Trade Center found the ashes helpful and said, "I choose to believe that a part of my brother's body is in these ashes" (Boss 2002). Other families want more. Family members have recently learned that of the 2,749 people killed at the Trade Center, more than 40 percent of the surviving families were given no identified remains of their loved ones, even though 40 acres of refuse that included body parts and possessions were taken to the City of New York's landfill. In 2003, Diane Horning, whose twenty-six-year-old son, Matthew, was killed at the Trade Center, founded the organization World Trade Center Families for Proper Burial to retrieve the remains from the landfill and give them proper burial. The organization represents about a thousand families (Berger 2008).

End the Process with Written Material

The notifier should provide written information before ending the death notification process. Because of grief, much of what has happened may not have been clearly understood by the family. Important details may be forgotten. It lessens stress to have basic information in writing, whether in a formalized document or handwritten by the notifier.

The written information can include details on how to contact a funeral home and what to expect from it. As always, sensitivity to the family's needs is essential. If the family is still significantly distraught and a visit to the home the next day is possible, it may be preferable to give them the written information at that time.

In cases involving criminal law, the written information should include autopsy information, how to obtain a crime report, the crime investigator's name and number, the prosecutor's name and number, and information about crime victim's compensation.

The following pages provide a sample template handout for families whose relative's death is potentially criminal in nature. When used, it should be adapted to the situation, the blanks should be filled in, and it should be printed on the appropriate letterhead. Sections not relevant to a particular case may simply be marked through.

Information for the Family of Victims of Crime

We are very sorry that your family is in so much emotional pain now and we want to do anything we can to help. It is difficult to think and make plans, so we hope the following information will be useful to you. Concern yourself only with the "For Now" section below. You can come back to the next section later. If you have questions about any of this information, feel free to call:

_____ at _____

For Now

- Your loved one has or will be taken to the Medical Examiner's Office in [city, state] _____, _____ for autopsy. Law following most unexpected deaths requires this medical procedure.

- The Medical Examiner's Office is open from [time]_____ until [time] _____, from _____ through [days of the week]. _____ Your loved one will be with them for a period of about 12 to 24 hours.

- Under some circumstances, the Medical Examiner allows family members to view loved ones before being taken to the funeral home. If you desire to do this, call _____ [job position] at [number] _____. Ask for a description of the condition of your loved one to help you decide if viewing is something you want to do.

- Be prepared to answer questions. The office may need further information from you in order to determine the exact cause of death.

- If you have not already selected a funeral home, you may want to ask a friend, relative, or your faith leader to contact several to compare costs and services and to be sure they accommodate spiritual rituals that are important to you.

- When a funeral home has been selected, call the Medical Examiner's Office at [number] _____ so they can arrange for transporting your loved one to the funeral home when their examination is complete.

- Your funeral home may contact you to make an appointment to discuss plans for the funeral and burial. Or you may contact them.

After the Funeral and Burial

- The officer conducting the investigation and preparing the investigation report is [name] _____ Please call him/her at [numbers] _____ if you have any further information about the crime or want to stay informed about the progress of the investigation.

- Your case number is _____. You may be able to obtain a brief report about the crime within a few days, but most of the investigation evidence must remain confidential until after the trial of the offender. To obtain the brief report, come to [name/address] _____
_____
between the hours of _____.
The fee for the report is $_____, payable by money order, personal check, or credit card. Call [number] _____ before going to the office to be sure the report has become available.

- For various tasks, you will need 6 or more copies of the death certificate, which the funeral home will obtain for you. They will be needed for Social Security benefits, Veteran's benefits, insurance benefits, access to bank accounts, some debt deletions, and other purposes.

- If you have an interest in reading the autopsy report, you may obtain it in approximately [amount of time] _____ by contacting [phone or address]._____ at _____. Fees may apply.

- You will need to contact the Social Security office to inform them of your loved one's death, unless the funeral home provides this service.

- If your loved one was a veteran, you will also need to notify the U.S. Department of Veterans Affairs. The phone numbers are:

  _____.

- You will need to inform your loved one's bank and insurance company(ies) of the death.

- If your loved one was murdered or killed by a drunk driver or by a hit-and-run driver, you may be eligible for financial help for medical and funeral costs, lost wages, and counseling that is not covered by your or your loved one's insurance. If you have not received an application from the hospital or the victim assistance office of the investigating police department or sheriff's office, please contact the Crime Victims Compensation Office at [number]

  _____.

  They are open [days/hours] _____.

- As long as the case is being investigated, you are entitled to crime victim services at no cost to you by calling [number] _____. They can inform you of your rights as a victim of crime, provide crisis counseling, and make referrals for ongoing services. They can also help you fill out the Victims Compensation Application and obtain the police report that must accompany the application.

- When your case is transferred to the prosecutor's office, similar victim services are provided. You should call [job position]

  _____

  at [number] _____ .

It is important to remember that this written information is a supplement to the personally delivered death notification and follow-up support of the notifier. The handout should not be a substitute for in-person death notification. Surviving family members need a personal, supportive, and compassionate notification process that is supplemented with the written, factual information in handouts like this sample.

As with every aspect of notification and follow-up, the family members' wishes will vary and all should be honored if at all possible.

Follow Up with the Family

The death notification process is still not finished until follow-up services are offered. These follow-up services speak volumes about the professionalism of your agency.

Make a Second Day Call

The day after the notification, the notifier should call the family and offer to visit with them again. If the family does not desire a personal visit, spend time with them on the phone and again express willingness to answer their questions. They will probably have many more questions than they did at the death notification itself.

Consider Delivery of Personal Items

The day after the notification is usually an appropriate time to ask the family if they are ready to receive their loved one's clothing, jewelry, and other personal items. It is best to honor their wishes if possible. They will need to be told if some or all of these things are being held as evidence until after a trial. If the clothing has been released, ask the family if they want to receive it as is, or if they prefer to have it laundered. (Most want it as is.) Clothing should be folded nicely and placed in a porous (like cardboard) box, not in a plastic trash bag. The clothing should be thoroughly dried to diminish offensive odors. If the family is ready to receive these things, the notifier should take them to the home, or if the family prefers, they can be held at an agreed-upon location for the family to collect. It is important to describe to the family what they will find in the box, and the condition of the items. Without this information, they may not be prepared for situations where the clothing has been cut off the body for treatment, or for clothing that contains blood and other body fluids. Jewelry may have become distorted or broken. ID may have been removed from wallets and purses to assist with the identification process.

This post-notification visit is also an opportunity to make sure that the family understands that a death certificate must be applied for in order for beneficiaries to receive the various benefits available to them. These benefits may include Social Security, federal and state Victim Compensation programs, and federal and state Workers' Compensation. Funeral homes usually assist with this process, but the family should inquire to be sure.

Attend the Funeral

Funeral attendance is another common follow-up concern of notifiers. If it is possible for the person who notified the family to attend the funeral, the family will probably be appreciative. Some notifiers worry that since they delivered the news of the death, family members may be upset by the notifier's presence. Experience suggests that this is rarely, if ever, true. Families appreciate the time and effort it takes to attend. This is particularly true when the notifier was with their loved one when he/she died for in this case, the notifier is the family's last direct link with their loved one.

Be Available for More Questions

Notifiers should be aware that family members may seek them out as more questions arise over the weeks, months, or even years after the death of their loved one. This is not unusual, especially if the death was unanticipated, and every effort should be made to accommodate such requests. The sudden death experience leaves families feeling somewhat like a jigsaw puzzle with pieces scattered all over the table. Over time, they need information to help them put those pieces together. Only then can they begin to make some meaning out of what happened.

The importance of patience with these recurring questions is illustrated by a story that a police sergeant who attended one of the MADD death notification trainings told.

Eight years ago, I investigated a fatal crash where a sixteen-year-old girl was killed. Being shorthanded, I requested the police department where her parents lived to make the death

notification. Someone from that department simply called them and told them to call our station. Our dispatcher didn't know what to do, so she told them to call the hospital. The hospital told them over the phone that their daughter had been killed. They were mad at me for the way the notification was handled, and I never understood why. Days later they wanted me to come to their house and tell them everything I knew. I didn't understand that either. Then about a year and a half later, the girl's younger sister showed up at the station and wanted me to tell her what happened. I still didn't understand why. Today I finally understand why.

Media Intervention

In some cases, media entities may attempt to discuss high-profile death cases with the notifier. If a dangerous offender is believed to be responsible for the death and is still at large, the public's safety and right to know may take precedence over the family's privacy. In this case, the public information officer of either the hospital or the investigative agency will probably make a statement about the death. It is prudent, in such cases, for the notifier to warn the family about the possibility of information being revealed over television, radio, or in the newspaper and to request that the public affairs officer tell the family before information about their loved one is released.

If the family wishes the notifier (or someone else) to serve as an intermediary between them and the media, every attempt should be made for the request to be honored. The notifier may need to refer the family to an appropriate media representative if the hospital or agency doesn't have one or if their intervention is only short-term. Victim services agencies or the victim advocate in law enforcement or prosecutors' offices are sometimes designated this role, but they generally represent their agency as well. They may be able to refer the family to an appropriate media representative in the community. This person's role involves regularly communicating with investigators and the prosecutor and informing the family about new developments so they do not hear it first through the media. If the media representative is in a position to make a statement on behalf of the family, the family should always approve the statement before it is distributed.

In criminal death cases, before making follow-up calls, the notifier should check with the law enforcement investigator to see if a suspect has been apprehended. If so, and if the family has not yet been informed of the arrest, the notifier may want to seek the investigator's permission to inform the family about whether charges have been filed and if the suspect is incarcerated or released on bail.

Most families are eager to get this information.

If the notifier is affiliated with the investigating agency or is familiar with the justice process, this follow-up call or visit provides an opportunity to correct misconceptions about the criminal justice system, especially information about why many suspects are released on bail. Suspects have the right to be free pending trial if certain criteria apply. These criteria include their being seen as no further danger to the community, being likely to appear for trial, and being able to pay bail. (This payment is usually 10 percent of bail amount set.) If the survivors express interest in attending a bail hearing, notifiers should encourage them to do so, especially if they know the suspect and have evidence that he or she may be a continuing threat or is likely to leave the area.

Experiential Exercises

Consider the following actual cases and answer the questions below each.

An adolescent boy was critically injured in a car crash, and his parents were called to the emergency department of their local hospital. The attending physician knew the boy had already died, but began the notification by describing his injuries in detail to the parents. He told them that their son had experienced very severe head injuries.
The mother cried out, "But can't you do something? Can't you operate?"
The physician responded, "Ma'am, if we opened up his head his brains would squish out like toothpaste out of a toothpaste tube."

- What impression do you think this made on the parents?
- With this beginning, how successful might the physician be in delivering the actual death notification compassionately?
- Why do you think the doctor told the mother what he did?
- How would you do it differently?

When a family returned home, they found their seventeen-year-old daughter unconscious in the den. They summoned Emergency Medical Services and the city police.

When the police arrived, the family was taken outside and not allowed back in. Two detectives arrived and went into the house. Shortly thereafter, one of the detectives came outside and asked the father what kind of relationship he had had with his daughter when she was alive. He then asked the father if he knew why someone might want her dead.

- How would you have reacted if you had been this father?
- Under what conditions should those who function primarily as investigators of a potential crime perform death notifications?
- How could this notification have been conducted differently?

A young man and his girlfriend were boating together over a Fourth of July weekend when another boat crashed into theirs, killing the young man. His mother lived in another state. To be sure that she was not notified by phone, the boating authorities at the lake asked the girlfriend for phone numbers of his mother's workplace, church, and a few friends. Calls to locate her were made without revealing the death. It was determined that she was at work. Her place of employment was called, and her supervisor was asked to notify her in person. Knowing that she was a person of faith, the supervisor first called her pastor. The pastor knew the mother's two best friends. He called them and drove to their homes to pick them up so that all three could notify the mother together. The mother is eternally grateful for this sensitive handling of her notification.

Point out aspects of this notification that worked well and why they worked well.

Summary

Specific guidelines on how to organize successful death notifications have been outlined, although notifiers are reminded that notifications never go as smoothly as planned. One must constantly be assessing which tools to use when, always with the twin goals of compassion and competency in the forefront.

Another very important component of follow-up has to do with the emotional health of the notifier. The death notification process is stressful, even for the most seasoned notifier. It is important for notifiers to talk about the experience with a trusted colleague or friend. This gives the notifier the opportunity to express his or her emotional reactions as well as to go over the facts of how the notification was handled (Lord 1997). Talking about how the notifier feels he or she did well or not well aids the strengthening of resilience following difficult death notification processes. Talking about such feelings and about the facts of the death notification also helps the notifier to plan for how to do the next notification similarly, or differently. More about the effects of death notification on the notifier is addressed in Chapter 3.

REFERENCES FOR CHAPTER 2

Awooner-Renner, S. 1993. I desperately needed to see my son. *British Medical Journal* 32:356.

Berger, R.M. 2008. At the hour of death. *Sojourners* 37, no. 2 (February), 27–31.

Boss, P. G. 2002. Ambiguous loss: Working with families of the missing. *Family Process* 41: 14–17.

Davis, J. 2003. Major tries to deliver hope when news is bad. *The Atlanta Journal-Constitution* (March 30), p. A-3.

Kaul, R. E. 2001. Coordinating the death notification process: The roles of the emergency room social worker and physician following a sudden death. *Brief Treatment and Crisis Intervention* 1:101–114.

Lord, J. H. 1997. *Death notification: Breaking the bad news with compassion for the survivor and care for the professional.* Washington, DC: U.S. Department of Justice, Office for Victims of Crime; and Irving, TX: Mothers Against Drunk Driving.

Lord, J. H. 2006. *No time for goodbyes: Coping with sorrow, anger, and injustice after a tragic death.* 6th ed. Burnsville, NC: Compassion Press.

McEwen, B. S. 2000. The neurobiology of stress: From serendipity to clinical relevance. *Brain Research* 886:172–189.

National Institutes of Health. 2007. Organ donation. Retrieved 6/3/07 from MedlinePlus, www.nlm.nih.gov/medlineplus/organdonation.html.

National Women's Health Information Center. 2007. Organ donation and transplantation. Retrieved 7/5/07 from http://womenshealth.gov/faq/organ_donation.htm.

Parrish, G. A., K. S. Holdren, J. J. Skiendzielewski, and O. A. Lumpkin. 1987. Emergency department experience with sudden death: A survey of survivors. *Annals of Emergency Medicine* 16:792–796.

Sanders, K., and M. Stavish. 1995. Wreck triggers double tragedy: Father dies after news of son's death in car. *Fort Worth Star-Telegram* (September 1), p. A1.

Sawyer, S. 1988. Support services to surviving families of line-of-duty deaths. Washington, DC: U.S. Department of Justice.

Schwartz, M. 2003. Investigating deaths in the field. *The Forum (Association of Death Education and Counseling)* 29 (3): 1, 3–4. Retrieved 2/29/08 from http://www.adec.org/publications/forum/0307.pdf.

Servaty-Seib, H. L., J. Peterson, and D. Spang. 2003. Notifying individual students of a death loss: Practical recommendations for schools and school counselors. *Death Studies* 27:167–186.

Stewart, A. E. 1999. Complicated bereavement and posttraumatic stress disorder following fatal car crashes: Recommendations for death notification practice. *Death Studies* 23:289–321.

U.S. Army. 1994. *Army casualty operations/assistance/insurance.* Army Regulation 600-8-1. Washington, DC: Department of the Army (October 20), 32. Available for download on 3/2/2008 at http://www.armystudyguide.com/content/publications/army_regulations/ar-60081.shtml.

U.S. Department of Health and Human Services. 2004. Mental health response to mass violence and terrorism: A training manual. Washington, DC: Substance Abuse and Mental Health Services Administration, Center for Mental Health Services.

Notes

3

Resilience Strategies for Notifiers

Death notification is inherently difficult. During the process, it involves emotionally laden multitasking as notifiers impart tragic information, manage reactions within themselves, and monitor the emotional reactions of the survivors.

Afterward, notifiers may feel drained and perhaps more vulnerable to the effects of their own losses. This may be especially true if there are similarities between the notifier's own life experiences and those of the family notified. In the case of a notification to parents about the death of their child, one similarity could be that the notifier is also a parent near the same age as the parents notified. Afterward, the first thing this notifier might want to do is go home and hug his own child, realizing anew how very vulnerable human life can be.

In this chapter, we address selection of notifiers, influences on death notifiers' immediate reactions to the process, strategies some notifiers have used to cope with performing death notifications, and suggestions for what notifiers can do to return to normal functioning after performing this important task.

A LAW ENFORCEMENT OFFICER'S PERSONAL REACTION TO A DEATH NOTIFICATION

Former Police Chief Wayne Smith of the Clatskanie, Oregon Police Department describes a death notification he delivered to parents following a fatal motor vehicle crash that killed their son. Chief Smith was a veteran notifier, but his experience is typical of what many notifiers face, both in terms of their own personal reactions and those of the surviving family.

As I approached the house I saw the mother and father standing in the driveway. I pulled into the driveway and my partner drove up behind me. I wasn't even out of the car when I saw the mom's lips begin to quiver. She started backing up and grabbed her face. Then she started screaming, "No! No! No!" Even though my patrol car windows were closed, I could hear her.

I've delivered many notifications, but for this one I was immediately full of anxiety. My stomach was in knots. I didn't want to do this—I wanted to find someone else to do it. These parents already knew why we were there. I tell you, I wanted to put the car in reverse and just back up and get out of there and say, "I don't want any part of this."

My partner must have felt the same way because he got on the radio and said, "I think you can handle this. I'll just go ahead and leave."

I told him, "No way! You're going in with me."

It was a very emotional scene. We got the parents inside. We spent a great deal of time with them, and then we had to go over and make the notification to her mother, where the son actually lived (with his grandmother). The grandmother ended up passing out on us, so we had to spend a lot of time there, too.

Chief Smith's experience illustrates several things that can affect your immediate and long-term reactions to death notification: (1) your personality and coping style, (2) your history of prior losses, and (3) the particular circumstances of a death notification (Bartone et al. 1982; Hodgkinson and Shepherd 1994). In this case, Chief Smith was a genuinely warm person who related well to people and generally handled stress appropriately. He had experienced no recent personal losses. He was conducting this assignment with a supportive partner, even though he, too, would like to have avoided the situation. Yet, there was something about seeing those parents in the driveway that triggered an emotional reaction in Chief Smith that he didn't expect. How they faced the death of their son was totally out of his control, and it was hard for him simply to let their emotions run their course.

SELECTION OF THE NOTIFIER

Selection of the notifier is as crucial as familiarity with the practices suggested in Chapter 2. In short, not everyone can be an effective death notifier in every situation. Yet it is often those who have delivered the most notifications and say they are unaffected by the task who are given the assignment. Those who deceive themselves into thinking that blocking emotion is being professional fail to recognize that emotions are as significant in the human experience as are thoughts and behaviors.

As discussed earlier, emotions can't control an investigator's interview with a witness or suspect. Nor can they control an emergency physician's attention to detail during a medical procedure. Emotions have their place, however, during a death notification as long as they do not overwhelm the notifier. A notifier's ability to relate emotionally to the family is important to them. They need to know the notifier cares. Notifiers who cannot care will not be effective. Feeling sad with the family is perfectly acceptable. They will be touched by compassion.

Sometimes the professional who no longer cares is simply overly stressed. Emergency physicians, paramedics and EMTs, law enforcement officers, and other crisis professionals are exposed to trauma every day. Dr. George Everly, a noted researcher on emergency services stress, estimates that at any given time 15 percent to 32 percent of emergency responders will be dealing with a posttraumatic stress reaction, and there is a 30 percent to 64 percent chance that they will have such a reaction sometime during their lifetimes (Everly and Flynn 2006). These reactions include intense fear, helplessness, or horror as well as intrusive symptoms such as recurrent and distressing recollections, avoidance symptoms such as trying hard not to think about it or feel about it, and physiological symptoms such as sleeping problems, hypervigilance, and an exaggerated startle response to unexpected sounds or sights. Noted posttrauma researcher Bessel van der Kolk points out that after dealing with too many death scenes over time, these events can replay in several ways: as thoughts and preoccupations, nightmares, flashbacks, body sensations, and behaving as if the event or events were happening all over again (van der Kolk 1991). Having to face grotesque sights and situations also has been identified as a predictor of traumatic stress reactions (Dunning and Silva 1980; Green et al. 1989). Too much involvement in gruesome or graphic death scenes can render professionals ineffective as death notifiers.

Although professionals with troubling reactions after viewing a gruesome death may be able to function well enough to perform some tasks, overly stressed individuals should not be assigned to make death notifications. If they were present when the death occurred, families may want to ask them questions, but addressing these questions can follow the actual notification.

The helplessness that professionals feel following a death they were unable to prevent is sometimes the trigger to posttraumatic stress. Unable to process the experience with customary coping mechanisms, they may feel numb—their body's way of attempting to deny the reality of what happened. This emotional paralysis alternates with waves of emotional reactions. A professional overwhelmed by this sense of helplessness may not be able to focus on the family during a death notification.

Officer-involved shootings, for example, are likely to produce posttraumatic stress. A study of the emotional, psychological, and physical reactions of 80 police officers and sheriff's deputies following 113 incidents in which they shot someone (Klinger 2006) revealed the following:

- Many officers found their recollection of the shooting to be inaccurate. Some could not recall firing their guns. Many suffered recurrent thoughts about it (83 percent), sleep interruption (48 percent), fatigue (46 percent), and anxiety (40 percent).

- Officers who experienced a lack of support from their colleagues and supervisors, or those who felt that aspects of the investigation were unfair or unprofessional, reported more severe and long-lasting negative reactions (lasting longer than three months) than those who felt supported.

Contrary to earlier research findings (Nielsen 1980; Stratton, Parker, and Snibbe 1987), however, few officers in the study suffered long-term negative consequences. The key factor that helped them regain their sense of normalcy was positive and supportive attitudes and behavior on the part of investigators, colleagues, family, and friends.

Those who do suffer long-lasting effects—who lose their ability to both give and receive in relationships also probably lose the sensitivity they need to be good death notifiers.

Experiential Exercises

Consider the following experience of Paul Reese, a firefighter who worked the Delta 191 airplane crash at Dallas/Fort Worth airport where 136 people were killed. Then answer the questions.

It was just unbelievable. I wasn't ready for what I saw—so many dead bodies and body parts. You couldn't see anything until you got right to it because it was raining so hard. I really didn't think I could make it into the plane without stepping on a person or parts of a person. I finally was able to pull some victims out. There was a lady on the concrete, incoherent. I could hear another one calling for help. I had to move one dead body out of the way to cut another man from his seatbelt. When I got to him, I could see that his leg was cut off and he was burned over 100 percent of his body. I saw three sets of legs—a man, a woman, and a child. When I turned the seats over, there was nothing but the legs. It was hard, putting the bodies in the body bags, knowing how many more there were to do.

Afterward, I developed a twitch in my left arm that came every time I went out on an alarm. It took a long time to stop. I still can't be out in a truck with low planes flying over me. I wonder if any of those people I pulled out survived. I wish there was some way to know who made it and who didn't.

- Should Paul be assigned to death notification duty?
- What physical reactions might he have when called upon to deliver a death notification?
- What emotional reactions might he have while delivering a death notification?
- What coping strategies might he choose, both healthy and unhealthy?

In summary, professionals suffering posttraumatic stress symptoms will not be comfortable or calm enough to deliver a compassionate death notification. Furthermore, asking them to do so is likely to exacerbate their own trauma reactions.

INFLUENCES ON THE IMMEDIATE REACTIONS OF NOTIFIERS

One of the earliest studies to identify personality characteristics of those who seem resilient to posttraumatic stress evaluated police, firefighters, and paramedics twenty months after the Delta 191 crash (Lanning 1987). Resiliency characteristics included the following.

- Easy-going personality and a sense of humor
- Adequate training

- Religious beliefs
- Opportunity to teach or train others
- Positive relationship with father
- Genuine desire to help people

Nielsen (1991) reviewed the literature on factors that are protective against posttraumatic stress disorder. He found (1) lack of physical problems, troubling emotional issues, relationship problems, and significant losses, and (2) positive social support. Even with these life circumstances, however, the nature of the traumatic event also weighed in heavily if the event was particularly disturbing.

RESEARCH ON HOW SOME NOTIFIERS MANAGE STRESS

Dealing with the stress of death notification, like dealing with other professional stressors, requires an active and organized approach. In the authors' study of death notifiers (Stewart, Lord, and Mercer 2000), we were interested in learning how notifiers actively coped with their notification experiences. We provided respondents with a list of ten stress-reducing activities and provided additional space for them to list their own unique strategies. Respondents rank-ordered the most useful strategies for them. A summary of these findings appears in Table 1 (See page 119).

Approximately 40 percent cited talking with coworkers as the single most helpful method for managing their stress after a notification, a trend also noted by Hodgkinson and Shepherd (1994). Spending time with family (26 percent) was in a distant second place, followed by spending time alone (24 percent).

There were no discernible differences based on professional affiliation (law enforcement, clergy, mortuary professionals, health care professionals, mental health professionals, and victim services providers), but differences did emerge according to gender. We found that more women talked with fellow workers (54 percent) than did men (31 percent). In addition, more men (33 percent) said they benefited by spending time with their families afterward than did women (19 percent). Slightly more men (16 percent) used exercise than women (10 percent). Although the top two methods of managing stress involved interpersonal communication (with coworkers or with family), interacting with friends outside of work was ranked much lower, regardless of gender or professional affiliation.

Spending time with these friends in other jobs ranked seventh for the total sample.

The use of coping strategies we observed in our sample was consistent with findings in a study of activities that therapists use to cope with their work-related trauma (McCann and Pearlman 1990).

COPING STRATEGIES THAT CAN HURT

Not all coping strategies are good ones. Unhealthy strategies may be deliberate, purely accidental, or developed out of what notifiers learned or witnessed in their original or immediate families. Some are simply bad habits. Regardless of their origin, however, it is important to recognize that the following can lead to problems if relied upon as long-term strategies, not only for coping with death notifications but also for coping with other professional and life stressors.

Denial

A commonly used defense is simply to deny the reality of the situations that are affecting you. Although denial may be somewhat useful as a short-term, intermediate step en route to recognizing the scope of your stress, it does not facilitate adjustment in the long term (Eth, Baron, and Pynoos 1987; Vaillant 1993). You may cope temporarily by denying the emotional impact of your trauma-related work, choosing to put off dealing with painful feelings until you are in a setting that you perceive as safe and supportive. This is an acceptable and adaptive use of denial for a little while. Repeatedly denying that your work is stressful, however, or denying that you are becoming more and more affected by the emotional outpourings of survivors during death notifications means that you never got around to processing—"unpacking"—your reactions.

Excessive denial is problematic simply because you cannot get away with it for very long. It is tempting to act as if painful life experiences can be put into a jar and kept there as long as the lid is screwed down tightly. Unfortunately, however, your mind and spirit are porous to feelings and will eventually find ways to express what you are trying to deny (Sternberg 2000). The price of denial can be increased susceptibility to illnesses or diseases such as gastrointestinal or heart problems, high blood pressure, sleep disorders, or increased bodily aches and pains, to name but a few symptoms (Sapolsky 1998; Sternberg 2000). If your characteristic coping style is to deny, discount, or minimize emotional reactions that arise within, you may benefit from a more extended examination of them, perhaps with the help of a professional therapist or psychologist.

Rationalization and Intellectualization

These strategies are less destructive than substance abuse, aggression, and suicide, but they still prevent you from authentic living (Vaillant 1993). Rationalization refers to the tendency to offer inaccurate explanations for behavior. You may behave one way, based upon an honest impulse or reaction, but then tell yourself and others that your behavior had a more socially acceptable motivation. For example, you may have been left feeling emotionally drained and unsettled after providing a death notification in a particularly tragic case. Instead of acknowledging your honest reactions and need for some rest, you make up a story about coming down with a cold or stomach virus as a way to stay home from work, take some time for yourself, and still save face.

Intellectualization is a cousin to rationalization that involves distancing yourself from your emotional reactions. A symptom of this defense is discussing stressful situations like losing a patient or delivering a death notification in an overly cognitive fashion. Here, people mask their honest reactions and put on a demeanor that is professionally detached, cold, aloof, or even clinical. Rather than exploring why a particular case is painful and what it means to the person who is involved in it, the person builds a barricade with words, concepts, and ideas.

Both rationalization and intellectualization are problematic to the extent that they abort more genuine reactions. Allowing genuine reactions to surface signals the opportunity to work through what happened and understand more about oneself.

Experiential Exercises

Read the following scenario and answer the questions following it.

A health care professional in a busy hospital emergency department walks into the waiting area and makes the following statement to the family that has gathered round. "The patient arrived in our department with multiple deep lacerations along with trauma to several vital organs. Because decreasing blood pressure and increased heart rate suggested pulmonary insufficiency, we instituted measures to revive the patient and to stabilize the heart. As the injuries were fatal in nature, our efforts at this treatment proved unsuccessful."

100

- What has the health professional just told the family?
- Do you think they understood it?
- How might the message have been communicated more appropriately?

Alcohol and Other Drugs

Sometimes, facing one's emotional reactions to work experiences is overwhelming. We all feel that way sometimes.

Relief from these feelings is readily available for some people through using or abusing alcohol or other drugs. This unhealthy strategy may be more common in people who have relatives, especially in their immediate families, who rely upon or have relied upon alcohol or other drugs.

The problems associated with using these substances as a long-term means for coping have been well documented and will not be reviewed here. (For more information, see, for example, Chermack and Giancola 1997; Holahan et al. 2001; Holahan et al. 2003). We will instead confine our comments to the ways that abusing drugs or alcohol can negatively affect coping with the stresses of work.

Although reactions to death notifications and other aspects of professional life can be painful and confusing, it is good to remember that feelings are primary ways of knowing. That is, feelings are the signals that give us important information about others and ourselves. Once we understand that feelings are trying to tell us something, we can try to understand the message and the painful feelings will probably decrease. For example, telling parents that their child has died or was killed is very emotionally painful. It should be. That pain can make you appreciate your own children more, recognize that we are all very vulnerable to death, and face the fact that it is unreasonable to think that life will always be fair and just. These truths are important to acknowledge. The pain of the notification is a valuable teacher.

Substances like drugs and alcohol dull our feelings and sensitivities so that our authentic emotions become muted and distorted. When this happens, the attention-getting functions of painful feelings become masked. The symptoms are medicated but the function of the emotional pain—to help us pay attention to something that needs attention—is negated. The tasks of genuine coping with the effects of death notifications and other painful life experiences are avoided. But feelings do not simply go away with time. The net result of using alcohol or other drugs to cope is that the pain can become even more intense and destructive when sober, and simultaneously, psychological and physical addiction begins. As more pain arises, so does your dependence on substances. In short, the strategy that was attempted as a solution becomes yet another problem.

How can you tell if you have a problem with alcohol or other drug use? First, think back over your life recently. Has anyone told you they think you have a problem with alcohol or other drugs? If you have received this feedback from someone you live with or even casually from a friend or professional acquaintance, then you may benefit from extended soul searching to assess how you may be relying (or overly relying) on substances.

Second, if you use alcohol or other drugs and are not sure if you are using them to a problematic extent, then try stopping cold turkey for one month. If you can remain abstinent for four weeks, then your use of substances may not be out of control. If you cannot remain abstinent for this period of time, then it is likely that you have a problem or dependence on one or more substances.

If you apply these two tests to your behavior, and you find that you have a problem or are not sure, then you may benefit from consulting a mental health professional who has experience in drug and alcohol assessment and treatment. In addition, you may benefit from attending a trial meeting of Alcoholics Anonymous or a similar 12-step program. Don't settle for less than the best treatment, however, because to do so increases your risk for relapse. Research on treatment has consistently shown that the longer the time in treatment, the better the outcome (Belenko 2000; Taxman and Bouffard 2003).

Experiential Exercises

Read the following scenario and answer the questions following it.

During World War II, Warren delivered death notification telegrams to families. He said that the emotional reactions of the families were so terrible that they were more than he could manage. Warren attributes the start of his substance abuse problems to those notifications.

- What might the military have done differently to make Warren's job easier for him?

- What might Warren have done differently to use healthier strategies for coping?

Angry or Aggressive Behavior

Sometimes sadness, sorrow, grief, or helplessness makes people feel very vulnerable and uncomfortable. They cannot tolerate these emotional reactions well. Instead of accepting them and attempting to work through the pain, they convert them to action. Almost like turning a switch, the sad feeling turns into anger or their behavior becomes aggressive. Being mad seems better than being sad because of the vulnerability that is part of being sad. The anger and aggression may seem like a way to correct or undo the situation that gave rise to the initial feeling.

Aggressive behavior can be especially damaging because it isolates people from others. When our words and behavior hurt others, they leave us alone. Who wants to stay around someone who becomes easily angry and blaming? Why would others want to take emotional and physical abuse?

We know that people can learn aggressive behavior by simply watching how others behave (Skoler et al. 1994). Witnessing our parents or older siblings acting aggressively can teach us to behave the same way (Conger et al. 2003). But when we shift gears that way, we fail to pay attention to the roots of the sadness. By behaving angrily and aggressively, we focus on someone else, often inappropriately blaming him or her for our hurt, sadness, and helplessness.

This rage, when unchecked, can have disastrous consequences. In June 2001, an eighteen-year career police officer shot and killed his wife, his two children, and himself. He had a history of isolation from his peers and of domestic arguments at home. The Denver Post (Robinson and Kelly 2001) said his department was puzzled as to why he had not obtained professional help before it was too late.

A self-assessment of angry or aggressive behavior is similar to that we outlined for substance use. If anyone has told you they think you have a problem with your anger or aggressive behavior, this may warrant a more extended examination of what is behind it. Similarly, if you know you are regularly using abusive, destructive language or acting physically aggressive toward people, things, animals, or other drivers on the highway, you may well benefit from assessment and therapy to help you change these tendencies. If you have ever had contact with the criminal justice system because of problems with your anger, it should function as an alarm for you to change how you deal with stress. If you don't, at the very least, you will spend a lot of time being lonely.

Substance Abuse and Aggression

It probably comes as no surprise that intimate partner violence and substance abuse tend to go hand in hand. Between 1993 and 1998, nearly three out of four victims who suffered violence by an intimate partner (a current or former spouse, boyfriend, or girlfriend) reported that alcohol or other drugs had been used when the violence was perpetrated on them (Greenfield and Henneberg 2001). Other researchers have found that one-fourth to one-half of men who commit acts of violence also have substance abuse problems (Center for Substance Abuse Treatment 1997). Either of these problems creates far more stress than they relieve. The combination of the two, however, is particularly lethal. If you fall into this category, you must seek immediate help, or recognize that you may lose your family and career, not to mention yourself.

Suicide

Suicide represents the ultimate in negative coping strategies, yet it is fairly common among crisis responders, particularly police officers. About 300 police officers in the United States commit suicide each year, compared with 140 to 160 who are killed in the line of duty (Honig and White 2000). The problems we have previously discussed, if unchecked, can progress to suicidal thoughts, planning how to take one's life, and eventually to carrying out one's suicide.

The most common risk factors for suicide among police officers are psychological difficulties, particularly traumatic stress, alcohol abuse, and relationship problems. Officers removed from service following a critical incident are also vulnerable. These issues, coupled with the availability of firearms, contribute significantly to the problem (Violanti 1996). If the stress you are experiencing has caused you to spend a lot of time thinking about your own death, or planning how you might accomplish it, remember that help is available. You must seek it immediately—either by telling someone you trust how much pain you are in or by seeking professional assistance. You may feel as if things can never get better. But they always can. Suicidal people have lost hope, but with help, the loss of hope becomes temporary. Suicide is permanent.

COPING STRATEGIES THAT CAN HELP

The strategies listed in Table 1 (See page 119) are by no means exhaustive of all the ways you and other professionals deal with the stresses of death notification in positive ways. In this section, we would like to help you brainstorm to find ways of coping that could work best for you.

Coping strategies are highly individualistic and can be best evaluated simply by how they work for you. Do they take you toward or away from mental and physical health?

In the sections below, we convey, in no particular order, suggestions for addressing the stresses of death notification that generally move people toward more resilient mental and physical health.

Obtain Death Notification Training

Paramedic Thomas Pechal spoke for thousands of notifiers when he said, "I learned the old-fashioned way. I watched and listened as my partner told the family that our patient was dead" (Pechal 2003).

If you have read this book up to this point, you are far ahead of Mr. Pechal. You have equipped yourself, in part, to handle some of the many scenarios that can be part of death notification work. To the extent that you can understand the concepts and adapt them to your particular work setting, you are reducing your chances of going into a death notification unprepared, having it go poorly, and then being affected negatively by it afterward.

In addition, when you use your own death notification knowledge and experiences to train colleagues and supervisees, you will help yourself even further. Knowing the recommended practices sufficiently well to present them to others in a training setting will enhance your own skills and confidence. Remember, however, that no amount of education in this area will allow you to perform this important duty without feeling the emotional effects of it. If it no longer hurts, you need to pass the duty to someone else. Knowing about the many aspects of death notification, however, is empowering.

Understand the Role of Your Previous Losses

A very specific influence on how you deal with death notification is the prior losses you have experienced. These losses include not only the deaths of relatives and friends, but also losses of family members or friendships through such events as divorce, relocation, children leaving home, changes in your physical health, and changes in your professional or occupational status. All these things give rise to feelings of loss and subsequent mourning. How you have dealt with such losses previously provides a good guide to how you will respond to performing death notifications.

If you recently have experienced one or more losses, then participating in death notifications could add to your overall sense of loss. This is especially true if the notification situation is similar to your own loss. If you find that you have been particularly affected or moved by performing a death notification, you could benefit from examining how the deceased's or the survivor's situation is similar to your own. You also may benefit, to the extent that it is possible, by taking a break from performing death notifications. This may mean that you ask for a more secondary role while others serve as the primary notifier.

If personal losses are affecting you significantly or continuously, then it is wise to obtain assistance from a trauma therapist or a grief counselor. A directory of trauma therapists can be found at the website for the International Society for Traumatic Stress Studies, http://www.istss.org. A similar listing can be obtained from the Association of Death Education and Counseling, http://www.adec. org.

Develop Your Personal Philosophy About Death

The work you do can heighten awareness of your own mortality. How you react during and after a death notification is affected by your personal philosophy about death. By philosophy, we do not mean an intellectual analysis or a formal philosophical system, but the views, attitudes, and beliefs you have developed about death throughout your lifetime. Although religion and spirituality are part of some notifiers' philosophies, others rely more upon their previous experiences, words of wisdom from supervisors or coworkers, or guidance from other sources.

How you develop your personal philosophy about death is less important than using or revising it into a meaningful framework for the work you do now. Some people who routinely deal with death adopt a kind of nihilistic philosophy stated in phrases like "death happens and you get over it." Although this may be true in a most elemental way, attitudes like this are symptoms either of an ill-defined personal philosophy of death or the denial of one's authentic reactions to death.

If you espouse such an orientation to death or have not yet developed a workable philosophy, your ability to relate effectively and supportively with survivors may be very limited. In addition, you may not have a good way to cope with the inevitable stresses that come with the notification process. A better strategy is to decide how you understand pain and suffering within the context of your work and what you do to diminish it as much as you can.

Explore or Enhance Your Religious and Spiritual Resources

Closely related to developing a personal philosophy of death is your reliance upon religious or spiritual resources. Trauma work can remind us all of the finiteness of life, of the fragility of human existence, and of how unforeseen, unexpected events can tragically end life. Most people want to be healthier and happier, have greater inner peace, and deal better with stress. Chang and Arkin (2002) show that increasing levels of affluence and materialism have failed to provide these intangible goals, but recent research shows that religiosity (defined as participating in faith-based services and rituals) and spirituality (defined as personal experience with the God of one's understanding) can contribute to a sense of well-being (Myers 2000; Pargament et al. 1990; Powell, Shahabi, and Thoresen 2003; Seeman et al. 2003).

You, too, may find that the faith you practice and the beliefs that you hold help keep your trauma work in a positive perspective. Talking with your priest, pastor, rabbi, imam, or other spiritual leader may help you feel better equipped to move forward in your work and personal life. By reading holy writings such as the Psalms you may find language to express your lament and anger for the pain and suffering in the world and discover new perspectives on death. As pastoral counselor Stephen Muse (2003) points out, "Tears and remembrance of injury in the presence of God and the witness of the saints who have faced similar pain are more healing than tears cried alone."

Many people find solace in attending or participating in religious services. The sense of community you experience with other worshipers may help you to feel that you are part of something bigger and more enduring that can restore you. People of faith tend to recognize that sharing God's love in every aspect of human life, with or without actually talking about religion, gives a new dimension to painful experiences. It strengthens their inner selves in the midst of chaos.

Seek Social Support

The stresses of trauma work and death notification can be reduced by relying upon the support, encouragement, and understanding that other positive people can provide. In fact, social support may be your single most important resource to cope with the stresses of life (Sternberg 2000; Lehman, Ellard, and Wortman 1986). We would like to note an important distinction between actual and perceived social support. Actual support pertains to the number of people with whom you are connected and from whom you draw support. Perceived social support is your perception of how much social support exists in your world regardless of the number of people you may know (Procidano and Heller 1983). The perception that people around you support you may be more important than the actual number of people with whom you are connected.

How you enlist people to help you cope with the effects of death notification or other professional stresses can vary widely. Because language is our primary means of sharing experiences, you will benefit from having someone with whom you can "be yourself" as you talk about important feelings and reactions. Psychologist Sidney Jourard refers to this as "the transparent self" (Jourard 1964). You may benefit from making a list of the people with whom you feel safe. These people appreciate your true self and do not judge you or exploit your vulnerabilities. You may also benefit from making a list of the emotionally toxic people in your life. These people judge you, drain you, and deplete your energy. You find yourself wanting distance from them when they are around. You do not have to be able to put your finger on what about them makes you uncomfortable—you just know you are. You will benefit from avoiding these people as much as you can.

People also vary in how they choose to seek doses of social support. You may benefit from lengthy decompression sessions with a friend or confidant. Or you may prefer taking a few minutes here and there to reveal and process your concerns. People who are natural extroverts are likely to enjoy more lengthy and detailed discussions with others than introverts who tend to benefit more from solitude than social interaction (Thorne 1987).

You probably will benefit from social support from both within and outside your family. By relying on their several kinds of relationships, you will receive the benefits of their varied life experiences. Even people who do not completely understand your work can listen attentively and offer a fresh perspective to your concerns. You may be surprised to learn that simply talking about yourself and your work in order to educate a friend about it will bring you a sense of relief, help you develop a new understanding of your issues, and help you realize that you actually are coping better than you thought you were.

Another reason to rely on people outside of your immediate family is that they may be better able to absorb some of your distress. Family members can become overburdened if you consistently share traumatic and stressful events with them. They may become ineffective in trying to support you because your problems have become their problems. They will need to seek support within their own support systems.

There is no one right way to share emotional reactions with another person. More important than how you talk about them is being in touch with the feelings inside and talking from this vantage point. This process is difficult for some people because of how they were raised in their own families and how their professional peers relate to them. Your subculture may erroneously tell you that a good officer, doctor, medical examiner, etc. can control emotional reactions without consequence. The traits most admired on the job—stoicism, analytic thinking, and a controlled demeanor—happen only when you suppress natural human reactions (Sugimoto 2003). The law enforcement community may be one of the most intimidating professions in this regard. One officer reported to the authors that when he once went to his supervisor to talk about a particularly painful death notification and began to cry, he was chastised with the question, "Are you going to be a snot-slinger your whole career?"

Police academies usually include a few sessions on psychological care, teach Crisis Incident Stress Management (CISM), and sometimes have chaplains and psychologists on staff. But the police subculture almost always has much greater influence on how officers ultimately choose to express themselves. Officers who seek counseling or psychological services may be stigmatized as weak or unstable, or their peers may even ostracize them. Even worse, their performance evaluations are often affected if they seek help (Sugimoto and Oltjenbruns 2001).

Getting past these hurdles is important for the sake of dealing with trauma-related stress. Making use of social support involves doing things with, as well as talking to, others. For instance, going out with friends for dinner or meeting at someone's home for a weekly activity can take your mind off your work and renew your faith in the goodness of life. One police officer pointed out that if he didn't routinely participate in such social opportunities, it wouldn't be long before he came to "feel like everybody in the world is either an asshole or a cop!" The regular presence of such friends can do much to make you feel that you are not alone and that there is a supportive force bigger than yourself, of which you are a part. This helps to keep the stressful parts of your professional life in a manageable perspective.

In a different vein, many people benefit from doing good deeds or providing for others (Monnier et al. 1998). By helping others, you come to feel more in control of yourself. You may not be able to control death or the surviving family's reactions, but you can control what you do with your own time.

Pursue Hobbies and Favorite Activities

Another way to restore yourself is to pursue hobbies or other activities you enjoy. By hobbies, we mean planned and organized ways of experiencing time, yourself, and other people in ways that are so enjoyable or meaningful that you become somewhat consumed with them. These are activities that you do not have to "work at." They come easily and effortlessly as you get into them. Regularly setting aside time and emotional space to pursue these activities has a decidedly positive effect on mental health (Csikszentmihalyi 1990). You owe it to yourself to engage in rejuvenating, replenishing, and restorative activities.

If you cannot think of what to try, think back to the things you enjoyed before you became so engaged in your work. Maybe you liked to go dancing or participated in an intramural sport, exercising, collecting memorabilia, creating works of art, writing, woodworking, cooking, or restoring cars. Performing stressful work, including death notifications, without taking time to take your mind totally away from it can lead to professional burnout. Even worse, it may accelerate into feelings of helplessness, hopelessness, or depression (Maslach and Leiter 1997).

Physical exercise is another good way to release the emotional and psychological tension that can accumulate after dealing with stressful situations like death notifications. Exercise can restore emotional balance because it converts tension into activity. Physical exercise can also jump-start coping responses by freeing the mind to consider new perspectives.

Some people do not have organized hobbies but pursue pastimes that perform the same psychological and emotional functions. These may include traveling, shopping, visiting museums, attending sporting events, going to the movies, attending plays, enjoying certain meals, getting massages, sitting in the whirlpool, or watching television.

There is no right way to assemble an enjoyable "cocktail" of hobbies or activities that refresh and restore you. The only requirement is that you genuinely enjoy what you do and pour yourself into it without feeling guilty or ashamed. To help you achieve success in this area and to expand your list of possible pursuits, we provide a list of enjoyable activities in Table 2 (See page 120).

Reduce Your Involvement in Delivering Death Notifications

Despite the availability of good coping resources, you may occasionally require extra time and space to renew yourself. If you are not coping well, consider reducing your involvement in death notification for a while. Many people who deliver death notifications, such as emergency department physicians, chaplains, medical examiners, or officers working in small law enforcement departments do not have the luxury of just not doing it. But in these circumstances, you may be able to identify another colleague or professional who may be willing to accompany you and to deliver the actual notifications, leaving you to function in a secondary or supportive role such as providing information after the notification.

The overall goal is to come up with an acceptable way to reduce your exposure to the distressing interactions that come with death notification work. Reducing your involvement in death notifications when they become burdensome is important so that you can avoid the exhaustion, detachment, helplessness and other symptoms associated with caregiver burnout (Wolfelt 1992), compassion fatigue (Figley 1995), or secondary posttraumatic stress disorder (Arzi, Solomon, and Dekel 2000).

CONCLUSION

Emotionally healthy death notifiers are effective because they know that behavior, thoughts, and emotional reactions are equally important. Although the suggested practices for performing a supportive and compassionate notification are rather straightforward, taking care of oneself in the aftermath may be even more challenging. Death notification work will always be difficult. But if you have not received training in how to do it, if you have not learned to examine your reactions to it, or if you find yourself choosing negative coping strategies, you can not only harm survivors you notify (even though not intentionally) but also hurt yourself and those you love as well.

If you care enough to absorb some part of the survivors' pain or trauma during a death notification, you must adopt a proactive role to care for yourself afterward. To help you take stock of how you may be doing overall, we offer a Death Notification Coping Strategy Checklist in Table 3. (See page121) This brief exercise will help you inventory both the positive and negative things you may be doing to cope with the stresses you experience personally, professionally, and especially following death notification work.

If you find that you have more positive, healthy strategies than negative ones, you are probably coping well and actually growing from the personal and professional challenges you resolve successfully. If you use more negative strategies, it is time to seriously consider making some changes in your life.

Madelyn Schwartz (2003), the medical examiner in Thurston County, Washington, describes the effects of healthy coping with death services this way:

I find myself hugging my daughter a lot, having well-defined boundaries, appreciating my connections with others, and driving slower ... The sense of connections with families I've notified, of having done and said the right things to help someone get through a truly heart-breaking ordeal, is profound. For all the God-awfulness, late hours, rushed meals, blood, stench, and ugly scenes, I don't want to do anything else.

REFERENCES FOR CHAPTER 3

Arzi, N. B., Z. Solomon, and R. Dekel. 2000. Secondary traumatization among wives of PTSD, and post-concussion casualties: Distress, caregiver burden, and psychological separation. *Brain Injury* 14:725–736.

Bartone, P. T., R. J. Ursano, K. M. Wright, L. H. Ingraham. 1989. The impact of a military air disaster on the health of assistance workers. *Journal of Nervous and Mental Disease* 177:317–328.

Belenko, S. 2000. *Statement made at hearing of the House Subcommittee on Criminal Justice, Drug Policy, and Human Resources*; Committee on Government Reform (April 4). In Drug treatment options for the justice system. U.S. Congress, House Journal. 106th Cong., 2nd sess., Hrg. No. 106-184; DTP 70-058. Retrieved on 3/3/08 from www.access.gpo.gov/congress/house/house07ch106.html.

Center for Substance Abuse Treatment. 1997. *Substance abuse treatment and domestic violence: Treatment improvement protocol (TIP) series 25*, prepared by Consensus Panel co-chairs P.A. Fazzone, J. K. Holton, and B. G. Reed. DHHS pubn. no. (SMA) 97-3163. Retrieved 3/3/08 from http://ncadi.samhsa.gov/govpubs/BKD239/default.aspx. Executive summary and recommendations retrieved on 3/308 from http://ncadi.samhsa.gov/govpubs/BKD239/25c.aspx.

Chang, L., and R. M. Arkin. 2002. Materialism as an attempt to cope with uncertainty. *Psychology & Marketing* 19:389–406.

Chermack, S. T., and P. R. Giancola. 1997. The relation between alcohol and aggression: An integrated biopsychosocial conceptualization. *Clinical Psychology Review* 17:621–649.

Conger, R. D., T. Neppl, K. J. Kim, and L. Scaramella. 2003. Angry and aggressive behavior across three generations: A prospective, longitudinal study of parents and children. *Journal of Abnormal Child Psychology* 31:143–160.

Csikszentmihalyi, M. 1990. *Flow: The psychology of optimal experience.* New York: Harper & Row.

Dunning, C., and M. Silva. 1980. Disaster-induced trauma in rescue workers. *International Journal of Victimology*, 5.

Eth, S., D. A. Baron, and R. S. Pynoos. 1987. Death notification. *Bulletin of the American Academy of Psychiatry Law* 15:275–281.

Everly, G. S. Jr., and B. Flynn. 2006. Principles and practical procedures for acute psychological first aid training for personnel without mental health experience. *International Journal of Emergency Mental Health* 8:93–100.

Figley, C. R., ed. 1995. *Compassion fatigue: Coping with secondary traumatic stress disorder in those who treat the traumatized.* Brunner/Mazel Psychosocial Stress Series. New York: Brunner/Mazel.

Green, B. L., J. D. Lindy, M. C. Grace, and G. C. Gleser. 1989. Multiple diagnoses in posttraumatic stress disorder: The role of war stressors. *Journal of Nervous and Mental Disease* 177:329–335.

Greenfield, L. A., and M. Henneberg. 2001. Victim and offender self-reports of alcohol involvement in crime. *Alcohol Research & Health* 25:21–22.

Hodgkinson, P. E., and M. A. Shepherd. 1994. The impact of disaster support work. *Journal of Traumatic Stress* 7:587–600.

Holahan, C. J., R. H. Moos, C. K. Holahan, R. C. Cronkite, and P. K. Randall. 2001. Drinking to cope, emotional distress, and alcohol use and abuse: A ten-year model. *Journal of Studies on Alcohol and Drugs* 62:190–198.

Holahan, C. J., R. H. Moos, C. K. Holahan, R. C. Cronkite, and P. K. Randall. 2003. Drinking to cope and alcohol use and abuse in unipolar depression: A 10-year model. *Journal of Abnormal Psychology* 112:159–165.

Honig, A. L., and E. K. White. 2000. By their own hand: Suicide among law enforcement personnel. *The Police Chief (October).*

Jourard, S. M. 1964. *The transparent self: Self-disclosure and well-being.* Princeton, NJ: Van Nostrand.

Klinger, D. 2006. Police responses to officer-involved shootings. *National Institute of Justice Journal (January), 253.*

Lanning, J. 1987. Post-trauma recovery of public safety workers for the Delta 191 crash: Debriefing, personal characteristics, and social systems. Unpublished; collection of the authors.

Lehman, E. R., J. H. Ellard, and C. B. Wortman. 1986. Social support for the bereaved: Recipients' and providers' perspectives on what is helpful. *Journal of Consulting and Clinical Psychology* 54:438–446.

Maslach, C., and M. P. Leiter. 1997. *The truth about burnout : How organizations cause personal stress and what to do about it*. San Francisco: Jossey-Bass.

McCann, I. L., and L. A. Pearlman. 1990. *Psychological trauma and the adult survivor: Theory, therapy, and transformation*. Brunner/Mazel Psychosocial Stress Series. Philadelphia: Brunner/Mazel.

Monnier, J., S. E. Hobfoll, C. L. Dunahoo, M. R. Hulsizer, and R. Johnson. 1998. There's more than rugged individualism in coping, part 2: Construct validity and further model testing. *Anxiety, Stress & Coping: An International Journal* 11:247–272.

Muse, S. 2003. Christ in our midst: Pastoral counseling from an Orthodox Christian perspective. *Journeys* 5:9,22.

Myers, D. G. 2000. *The American paradox: Spiritual hunger in an age of plenty*. New Haven: Yale University Press.

Nielsen, E. 1980. *Post-shooting reactions and deadly force policies*. PhD diss., University of Utah.

Nielsen, E. 1991. Factors influencing the nature of posttraumatic stress disorders. In *Critical incidents in policing*, ed. J. T. Reese, J. M. Horne, and D. Dunning, 213–219. Rev. ed. Washington, DC: U.S. Dept. of Justice, Federal Bureau of Investigation.

Pargament, K. I., D. S. Ensing, K. Falgout, H. Olsen, B. Reilly, K. Van Haitsma, and Richard Warren. 1990. God help me (I): Religious coping efforts as predictors of the outcomes to significant negative life events. *American Journal of Community Psychology* 18:793–824.

Pechal, T. 2003. Emergency rescue workers dealing with death. *The Forum (Association of Death Education and Counseling)* 29 (3): 5. Retrieved 2/29/08 from http://www.adec.org/publications/forum/0307.pdf.

Powell, L. H., L. Shahabi, and C. E. Thoresen. 2003. Religion and spirituality: Linkages to physical health. *American Psychologist* 58:36–52.

Procidano, M. E., and K. Heller. 1983. Measures of perceived social support from friends and family: Three validation studies. *American Journal of Community Psychology* 11:1–24.

Robinson, M., and S. Kelly. 2001. Murder-suicide baffles family, force: Police wondering why officer didn't seek counseling. *The Denver Post* (June 24), p. 2B.

Sapolsky, R. M. 1998. *Why zebras don't get ulcers: An updated guide to stress, stress-related diseases, and coping.* New York: W. H. Freeman.

Schwartz, M. 2003. Investigating deaths in the field. *The Forum (Association for Death Education and Counseling)* 29 (3): 1, 3–4. Retrieved 2/29/08 from http://www.adec.org/publications/forum/0307.pdf.

Seeman, T. E., L. F. Dubin, L. Fagan, and M. Seeman. 2003. Religiosity/spirituality and health: A critical review of the evidence for biological pathways. *American Psychologist* 58:53–63.

Skoler, G. D., A. Bandura, D. Ross, S. A. Ross, and R. A. Baron. 1994. Aggression. In *Readings in social psychology: General, classic, and contemporary selections*, ed. W. A. Lesko, 296–326. Needham Heights, MA: Allyn & Bacon.

Sternberg, E. M. 2000. *The balance within: The science connecting health and emotions.* New York: W. H. Freeman.

Stewart, A. E., J. H. Lord, and D. L. Mercer. 2000. A survey of professionals' training and experiences in delivering death notifications. *Death Studies* 24:611–631.

Stratton, J., D. Parker, and J. Snibbe. 1987. Post- traumatic stress disorder and the perennial stress-diathesis controversy. *Journal of Nervous and Mental Disease* 175:5.

Sugimoto, J. D. 2003. Death encounters in law enforcement. *The Forum (Association for Death Education and Counseling)* 29 (3): 6.

Sugimoto, J.D., and K. A. Oltjenbruns. 2001. The environment of death and its influence on police officers in the United States. *OMEGA: Journal of Death and Dying*, 43:145–155.

Taxman, F. S., and J. A. Bouffard. 2003. Substance abuse counselor's treatment philosophy and the content of treatment services provided to offenders in drug court programs. Manuscript cited at the Substance-abusing Offender Focus Group forum (July 24–25) sponsored by U.S. Department of Justice, the Bureau of Justice Assistance, Washington, DC.

Thorne, A. 1987. The press of personality: a study of conversations between introverts and extraverts. *Journal of Personality and Social Psychology* 53:718–726.

Vaillant, G. E. 1993. *Wisdom of the ego.* Cambridge, MA: Harvard University Press.

van der Kolk, B. (1991). The psychological processing of traumatic events: the personal experience of posttraumatic stress disorder. *Critical incidents in policing*, ed. J. T. Reese, J. M. Horne, and D. Dunning, 359–364). Rev. ed. Washington, DC: U.S. Dept. of Justice, Federal Bureau of Investigation.

Violanti, J. M. 1996. *Police suicide: Epidemic in blue.* Springfield, IL: Charles C. Thomas.

Wolfelt, A. 1992. *Understanding grief: Helping yourself heal.* New York: Routledge.

Notes

Appendix

TABLE 1

Strategies Used to Manage Death Notification
and Related Bereavement Work (Stewart, Lord, and Mercer 2000)

STRATEGY	Number of Persons and Percentage Using Each Strategy		
	Males	Females	Total Sample
1. Talk with fellow workers	33 (31%)**	31 (54%)	75 (40%)
2. Spend time with family	33 (33%)	11(19%)	47 (26%)
3. Spend time alone	23 (25%)	12 (23%)	40 (24%)
4. Exercise	13 (16%)	5 (10%)	21 (14%)
5 Attend religious services	8 (11%)	5 (12%)	15 (11%)
6. Spend time pursuing hobbies	8 (9%)	4 (8%)	12 (7%)
7. Interact with friends outside of work	3 (3%)	2 (4%)	7 (4%)
8. Pamper self	1 (1%)	8 (7%)	9 (8%)
9. Practice yoga or meditation	6 (7%)	0 (0%)	6 (7%)

Notes: The frequency of each strategy is based upon the number of times that the strategy was ranked #1 (i. e., used most frequently).

** The percentages are based upon the number of persons who responded to each stress management strategy. The number of persons who ranked the strategies ranged from 107 (attending religious services) to 188 (talking with coworkers).

TABLE 2

Some Suggestions for Enjoyable and Restorative Activities:

1. Telephone or visit a friend.
2. Listen to your favorite music (from the past or the present).
3. Go hiking or take a walk in a scenic or natural area.
4. Make a list of all that you have accomplished over the last year.
5. Remind yourself of what you have accomplished.
6. Take a ride on your bicycle.
7. Go to a nonviolent movie or watch a funny video.
8. Read (or reread) a book by your favorite author.
9. Swap books with those of a good friend, read them, and discuss them.
10. Make or buy a gift for someone.
11. Work in your flower or vegetable garden.
12. Write a letter to an old or close friend. Thank them for their friendship.
13. Spend some time observing nature or visit some scenic natural sites.
14. Spend a day or weekend doing helpful things for others.
15. Attend seminars or classes offered through community or vocational schools. (Some are free.)
16. Attend weekend classes on cooking or wine tasting.
17. Clean, straighten, or reorganize a room, closet, or work area.
18. Go to a busy and public place, order an enjoyable beverage, and then sit and watch the people and events that just happen for a while.
19. Be a tourist in your hometown and discover something you haven't seen yet.
20. Find a secluded and peaceful outdoor area to go and think for a while.
21. Read a funny book, visit the website of a comedian, or read a book of jokes.
22. Wash and wax your car and take it out for a drive on a sunny day.
23. Plan a weekend getaway to a favorite or scenic spot (e. g., to see the fall leaves).
24. Feed your senses by sitting and taking in pleasant smells of freshly cut grass, the first wood fires from fireplaces in the fall, the ocean air, a cold winter morning, and the first barbecue in the spring.
25. Spend some time with your pet. Take your dog for a walk or play with your cat.
26. Go to a park or playground and watch children play. Appreciate their innocence and listen to them laugh.
27. Go into a church, synagogue, or mosque and sit for a while, being open to your own sense of spirituality.
28. Contact an old friend you haven't seen for a long time.

TABLE 3

Death Notification Coping Strategy Checklist

Instructions: For each strategy in the positive and negative columns, use the scale below to indicate how frequently you use the strategy. Also, note that you can add your own positive and negative strategies to the list. When you have rated all of the strategies, calculate the total of the ratings and then divide by the number of strategies that you rated. A higher average for the positive column indicates that you more frequently rely upon positive, healthy strategies. Alternatively, a higher average score for the negative strategies suggests that you tend to cope with stress in a less healthy manner.

0 = I never use this strategy
1 = I use this strategy infrequently or rarely
2 = I use this strategy sometimes or occasionally
3 = I use this strategy frequently or often
4 = I always use this strategy

Positive Strategies
_____ Obtain death notification training
_____ Develop a personal philosophy of death
_____ Utilize spiritual or religious resources
_____ Seek social support
_____ Pursue hobbies and favorite activities
_____ Other: _____

_____ **Total Positive Strategies**
_____ Average (Total divided by number of strategies rated)

Negative Strategies
_____ Engage in denial (other than temporary)
_____ Use rationalization/intellectualization
_____ Rely on substance use to calm yourself
_____ Behave angrily or aggressively (verbally or physically)
_____ Have suicidal thoughts and consider acting on them
_____ Other: _____

_____ **Total Negative Strategies**
_____ Average (Total divided by number of strategies rated)

Notes

Resources

American Association of Suicidology
www.suicidology.org
5221 Wisconsin Avenue, NW, Washington, DC 20015
202-237-2280 / 800-273-TALK (8255)
202-237-2282 (fax)

Compassionate Friends
www.compassionatefriends.com
P.O. Box 3696, Oak Brook, IL 60522-3696
630-990-0010 / 877-969-0010
630-990-0246 (fax)

Concerns of Police Survivors (COPS)
www.nationalcops.org
P.O. Box 3199
South Highway Five, Camdenton, MO 65020
573-346-4911
573-346-1414 (fax)

Mothers Against Drunk Driving (MADD)
www.madd.org
511 E. John Carpenter Fwy. #700, Irving, TX 75062
877-MADD-HELP • 972-869-2206 (fax)

Parents of Murdered Children
www.pomc.com
100 E. 8th Street, B-41, Cincinnati, OH 45202
513-721-5683 / 888-818-POMC
513-345-4489 (fax)

Tragedy Assistance Program for Survivors (TAPS)
(for military deaths) www.taps.org
1621 Connecticut Avenue, NW, Suite 300
Washington, DC 20009
202-588-TAPS (8277) / 800-959-TAPS (8277)

NATIONAL ORGANIZATIONS THAT HELP ALL VICTIMS OF CRIME (INCLUDING FAMILIES OF THOSE KILLED)

**National Association of Crime
Victim Compensation Boards**
www.nacvcb.org
P.O. Box 7054, Alexandria, VA 22307
703-780-3200
703-780-3261 (fax)

National Center for Victims of Crime
www.ncvc.org
2000 M Street, NW, Suite 480, Washington, DC 20006
202-467-8700 / 800-FYI-CALL
202-467-8701

National Organization for Victim Assistance (NOVA)
http://www.trynova.org
Courthouse Square
510 King Street, Suite 424, Alexandria, VA 22314
703-535-6682 / 800-TRY-NOVA
703-535-5500 (fax)

National Sheriff's Association (Victim Program)
www.sheriffs.org
1450 Duke Street, Alexandria, VA 22314
703-836-7827
703-683-6541 (fax)

Office for Victims of Crime (OVC)
www.ovc.gov
U.S. Department of Justice
810 Seventh Street, NW, Washington, DC 20531
202-307-5983 • 202-305-2446 (fax)

Office for Victims of Crime Resource Center
www.ojp.usdoj.gov/ovc/ovcres
National Criminal Justice Reference Service
P. O. Box 6000
Rockville, MD 20849-6000
800-851-3420

NATIONAL TRAUMA AND BEREAVEMENT COUNSELING ORGANIZATIONS

American Psychological Association
www.apa.org
750 First Street, NE, Washington, DC 22002-4242
202-336-5500 / 800-374-2721

Association for Death Education and Counseling (ADEC)
http://www.adec.org
111 Deer Lake Road, Suite 100
Deerfield, IL 60015
847-509-0403
847-480-9282 (fax)

Association of Traumatic Stress Specialists
http://www.atss.info
P.O. Box 246, Phillips, ME 04966
800-991-ATSS (2877)
207-639-2434 (fax)

Center for Loss and Life Transition
www.centerforloss.com
3735 Broken Bow Road, Fort Collins, CO 80526
(970) 226-6050
800-922-6051 (fax)

International Society for Traumatic Stress Studies
http://www.istss.org
111 Deer Lake Road, Suite 100
Deerfield, IL 60015
847-480-9028
847-480-9282 (fax)

National Crime Victims Research and Treatment Center
www.musc.edu/cvc
Medical University of South Carolina
P.O. Box 250852, Charleston, SC 29425
843-792-2945
843-792-3388 (fax)

NATIONAL RESOURCES FOR CIVIL SUITS

National Crime Victim Law Institute
www.ncvli.org
10015 SW Terwilliger Blvd., Portland, OR 97219
503-768-6819
503-768-6671 (fax)

Trial Lawyers for Public Justice, P.C.
www.tlpj.org
1717 Massachusetts Avenue, NW, Suite 800
Washington, DC 20036
202-232-7203 (fax)

Victim's Assistance Legal Organization (VALOR)
www.valor-national.org
8180 Greensboro Drive, Suite 1070, McLean, VA 22102-3823
703-748-0811
703-245-9961 (fax)

NATIONAL MEDICAL RESOURCES

American College of Emergency Physicians
www.acep.org
1125 Executive Circle, Irving, TX 75038-2522
972-550-0911 / 800-798-1822
972-580-2816 (fax)

American Trauma Society
http://www.amtrauma.org
7611 So. Osborne Road, Suite 202, Upper Marlboro, MD 20772
800-556-7890
301-574-4301 (fax)

Brain Injury Association of America
www.biausa.org
1608 Spring Hill Road, Suite 110, Vienna, VA 22182
703-761-0750
703-761-0755 (fax)

Spinal Cord Society
19051 County Hwy 1
Fergus Falls, MN 56537-7609
218-739-5252
218-739-5262 (fax)

NATIONAL FUNERAL/BURIAL ORGANIZATIONS

National Funeral Directors Association
www.nfda.org
13625 Bishop's Drive
Brookfield, WI 53005
262-789-1880/800-228-6332
262-789-6997 (fax)

INDEX

About the Authors

JANICE HARRIS LORD

Janice Harris Lord remembers the first death notification she received as a four-year-old child. She knew that her Uncle Francis, who adored her, had died in a car crash and that everyone around her was sad. However, she wasn't sure what "died" meant. When she saw him in his casket, she thought he was simply asleep. No one talked with her further about it. Details about his death remain a mystery to her.

Much later, in 1982, Janice became National Director of Victim Services for Mothers Against Drunk Driving (MADD). Noting little more than the Cocoanut Grove fire in the professional literature, she began calling families in which someone had been killed or injured by a drunk driver. She asked them to share their stories with her. Over and over again, they talked about their death notifications. Most had been delivered by phone, and even those that were personally delivered tended to be formal, cold, and lacking in compassion.

Several years later, Ms. Lord received funding from the Office for Victims of Crime (OVC), U.S. Department of Justice, to research and design a curriculum on death notification. The following year, OVC funded four versions of the curriculum—one each for law enforcement workers, health care professionals and medical examiners, clergy and funeral directors, and victim advocates. These curricula enabled training sessions to be offered all over the country by MADD. The evaluations of those training sessions led to Alan Stewart's research.

Janice Harris Lord is a licensed social worker, professional counselor, and private consultant on crime victim issues. She is a Fellow in Thanatology with the Association of Death Education and Counseling (ADEC) and a member of International Society of Traumatic Stress Studies. Ms. Lord has a broad work background focusing on homicide, catastrophic injury, death notification, standards and ethics in victim services, and spiritually sensitive victim services.

She has presented on these and other topics at the national, regional, and state levels.

Ms. Lord has authored numerous publications including the new and revised sixth edition of her book *No Time for Goodbyes: Coping with Sorrow, Anger and Injustice After a Tragic Death* in 2006 and *Spiritually Sensitive Caregiving: A Multi-Faith Handbook* in 2008. She has received national recognition, including a commendation for Outstanding Services in Crime Victim Advocacy, presented by U.S. Attorney General Janet Reno for President Clinton in 1993.

Alan E. Stewart

Alan E. Stewart also has personal experience with sudden, untimely, and tragic death. Two of his cousins were killed in vehicular crashes—Keith Emerson Clarke in 1972 and Danny B. Newton in 1980. The memories of these losses remain vivid and form the emotional inspiration for Stewart's work in death notification. In addition, when he was growing up, Alan and his father searched salvage yards for parts to restore their project cars. Stewart could not help but wonder what happened to the people and families who had been in the badly wrecked vehicles. Thoughts that began with, "Did someone die in here?" soon gave way to questions like, "Did someone have to tell the family that their loved one would not be coming home?"

Stewart began studying death, loss, and trauma while completing a research postdoctoral fellowship in the psychology department at the University of Memphis under the direction of Professor Robert A. Neimeyer. He received his PhD in counseling psychology from the University of Georgia in 1994. He is an associate professor in the Department of Counseling and Human Development at the University of Georgia, and also the coordinator of the Community Counseling master's program.

Alan E. Stewart is a board member of the American Society of Victimology and was honored by the ASV in 2007 with the John P. J. Dussich Award for research in victimology for his work in death notification. Stewart has published numerous journal articles, book chapters, encyclopedia entries, and other works on the topics of death, loss, and trauma.

Order Form

I'll Never Forget Those Words: A Practical Guide to Death Notification can be ordered by check, money order, Visa, or Mastercard.

Mail or fax this form, or call: **800-970-4220** to place your order.
For orders outside the U.S. call: **828-675-5909**
You can also order on our secure website, **www.compassionbooks.com**

1-9 copies: $12.95 each • 10-19 copies: $9.72 each (25% discount)
20 or more copies: $7.77 each (40% discount)

Shipping:
1 copy: $3.50 • 2 - 9 copies: add $.50 additional postage for each copy.
10 copies or more, add 10% of total

Place my order for _____ copies of: *I'll Never Forget Those Words*

@ $_____ each = $ _____

Tax (NC only) 6.75%: _____

Shipping: _____

Total of check or money order for: $ _____
Make checks payable to: **Compassion Books, Inc.**

Please charge my credit card (Visa or MC only)
Card # _____Exp. date _____
V#_____ (last 3 digits on back of card at end of signature strip)

Ship To (Name): _____
Organization: _____
Address:_____
City/State/ Zip:_____
Phone :_____Fax: _____

Mail or Fax your order to: Compassion Books, Inc.
7036 State Hwy. 80 South Burnsville, NC 28714

1-800-970-4220 / (828-675-5909) or Fax: 828-675-9687
email: orders@compassionbooks.com • www.compassionbooks.com

For hundreds of carefully chosen resources to help with
grief and loss, comfort, hope, and healing
visit our website at
www.compassionbooks.com